Praise for

THE POWER OF MOMENTS / SHAWN TRAUTMAN

"Shawn sees people in ways they often don't see themselves."
When I told him I used the back door because the front was for important guests, he said, 'Then I'd like you to come to the front door next time.' It was more than kindness—it shifted how I saw my own worth. **That's the kind of impact he makes—with moments most would miss.**
— *B. Hadley, Compassion Specialist*

"He doesn't miss his kids' events—and that spoke volumes."
I met Shawn on the golf course, following his daughter in a high school match. What stood out even more was how deeply he's rooted in his family and community. **I'm grateful God crossed our paths that sunny afternoon.**
— *T. Branscum, Servant Leader in Action*

"His presence invites you to slow down, engage differently, and notice what matters."
Over the years, I've seen Shawn influence nearly everyone he connects with—not by telling, but by helping people see their own value. What felt like casual conversations often stayed with me—**because they sparked reflection and growth.**
— *S. Steiner, Brand Strategist & Leadership Consultant*

"His stories ground me, humble me, and always lead to reflection."
Shawn has a way of inviting the reader into new perspectives. **I walk away with more clarity—and a deeper desire to grow, not just for myself, but for others too.**
— *O. Clark, Coach & Community Leader*

"Shawn's writing transports you into his world."
He draws such clear pictures with his words that you immediately see what he's seeing and feel what he's feeling. **And when it's over, you're just grateful he told the story.**
— *K. Arehart, Real Estate Agent*

"The Power of Moments is a collection of snapshots from a life that makes the most of each one."
I've never met anyone like Shawn, who inspires me to be a better human by packing value into every minute of almost every situation. **I'm envious of his discipline to slow down, ask questions, and place such high value on these moments that he sees them as worth writing down.** His words made me laugh out loud, smile, tear up—and think. **At the end of each chapter, he quietly challenges you to reflect on your own life.**
— *J. Bader, Leadership Development Advisor*

"A dead end is only a dead end if you stop."
Clarity and gratitude run through all of Shawn's work—
But that line might be the best description of his writing, his attitude, and his life that I've ever heard.
— *A. Milby, Success Coach*

"Shawn changed my life with his calm wisdom, supportive guidance, and ability to help me see problems differently."
His way of breaking down the everyday stress of modern life into something manageable is both simple and revolutionary. **Thanks to his perspective, I carry less stress and more compassion into my days.** This book gently invites you to shift your viewpoint—to sit in a different chair, so to speak—and try responding in a new way. Not to confront or relive the past, but to ask yourself: What if I never mentioned that again? What if I tried to find common ground instead?
— *S. Austin, Editor & Team Building Champion*

"There are moments in Shawn's stories that make me stop and think—this is real life."
His writing is full of feeling and always keeps me engaged. He inspires me with the way he tells the truth through story—and makes it feel personal.
— *M. Compton, Team Leader & Coach*

SHAWN TRAUTMAN

"THERE ARE DEFINING MOMENTS IN ALL OUR LIVES AND YOU'VE CAPTURED THEM HERE BRILLIANTLY!"
– M. BRANSON

THE
POWER OF
MOMENTS

BECAUSE EVERY MOMENT TELLS A STORY
—AND EVERY STORY HOLDS A LESSON

(Available in paperback & ebook wherever books are sold)

Written by: Shawn Trautman
Published by: Feel Good Books

This book is dedicated to those of you who still believe in humanity and are out there making the world a better place...
I see you and support your mission!

SHAWN TRAUTMAN

"THERE ARE DEFINING MOMENTS IN ALL OUR LIVES AND YOU'VE CAPTURED THEM HERE BRILLIANTLY!"
– M. BRANSON

THE
POWER OF
MOMENTS

BECAUSE EVERY MOMENT TELLS A STORY
——AND EVERY STORY HOLDS A LESSON

Thank you ALL for your encouragement and support!
- With love, respect & gratitude.

HOW TO USE THIS BOOK

"Read this before you <u>read this...</u>"

Every moment tells a story. Every story holds a lesson. And that's why this book, as a hybrid of inspirational stories and empowering actions has the potential to truly stand out—like a goldfish among shiners.

I'm a storyteller by nature, but I'm also a guy who loves teaching moments. Doesn't matter what I'm doing, I look for applicable story lines to help teach whatever it is I'm teaching as the two go hand-in-hand. So when I first completed this book I was thrilled as these stories needed to be told. But when I looked closer on my second read-through I found a gap.

The gap I found was for leaders who might want more. It's for educators who might say, "So what can we do with this?" Or, even better, "How do I apply this in my own life?"

When I took that perspective, I went back and dug deeper on every story so I could help move the needle from "just a story" to "a story with purpose." I wanted to add more context to the stories and help frame them for people **IF** (that's an important IF) they wanted to apply it in their own lives. I just didn't want to disrupt the flow of the book.

If you know me, you know this was a challenge—a MAJOR challenge. How do I keep managers interested, but also provide details for coaches who want more? Oy.

So what I did was this. At the end of each chapter I added a section that's called MAKING IT MATTER. It's **optional**. As in, you **don't have to read it** unless you want to. The stories by themselves are standalone experiences and they'll matter to you in whatever capacity you perceive them.

But if you want more context—a summary, some truths the story helps uncover, some actions you can take **if** you want to, and some questions to ask yourself—please be my guest and take yourself down your own self-help journey.

I added that section with the intent to **help, not hinder** so please don't let it weigh you down or make you feel overwhelmed in any way. And, to make the book easier to follow, I made sure the MAKING IT MATTER section kept to a predictable format—especially on the "Bringing It Home" part where I tried to give an immediate action (as in, today), a short-term action you could do (as in, this week), and a mid-term action you could do if you wanted to (as in, by the end of the month).

And, let's be honest: my advice is *my advice* as though I'm talking to a friend—because I am. I'm not a doctor nor some self-help guru, but I do have a lifetime of experience in leadership and connecting with people, reflecting in ways that matter, and teaching with the intent of helping others improve their lives. And I truly believe it will help you if you want to have greater impact and make more meaningful moments happen in your own life—often, for others.

Again, you're welcome to skip the MAKING IT MATTER section if you prefer **OR** you can join in and take yourself in all sorts of new directions related to your thoughts and actions going forward.

With that, welcome to **The Power of Moments,** where I aim to engage, entertain, and get you to think in ways you might never see otherwise.

These are all real stories of my life—extraordinary things that have happened to me, remarkable people I've met, and incredible experiences I've been fortunate enough to be a part of. Stories I hand-picked and worked through to ensure a wide-variety of topics could be explored—each with lessons I wanted to convey.

My hope is that these stories resonate with you on a deep level, allow you to see things from a different perspective, and help you look at your own **moments** in a whole new way.

Thank you so much for being here and joining me. Without an audience, stories lose their meaning and we just kinda' drift our way to the end. I'd like mine to mean something more, and if even one of my stories helps you in your life then I feel like this part of my journey has been time well spent.

That's it! I'm ready if you are. Let's do this together—just rest assured I'm on your team. Now let's go make something great of the time we still have left.

Wishing you the best, always,

01

MY WAY

My mind was spinning.

Did that really happen?

What does this mean for me?

How do I move forward and do things my way?

These were just some of the questions I had that night—while on a red-eye from LaGuardia Airport to Tampa, FL.

Sixteen hours earlier, I was on my way from Tampa to New York City and my questions were completely different.

Is this guy for real? Will I recognize him when I see him? What's the plan for the day? Where will we be going? How will it turn out?

For three months prior to this day we'd only talked through email and over the phone. He wanted to meet in person and have a heart-to-heart conversation about the entertainment industry. He said there were things I should know that he'd reveal in person only and that we should meet.

The mystery part was there. So was the intrigue.

At the time, my company was about five years old. We were building a brand and had just helped launch the pilot book of a series that had huge aspirations, had twenty-five full-length DVDs on the market, and had several best sellers on Amazon.

So what could this guy do and what is his background?

The way it was presented to me by a co-worker named Amanda was that this guy was one of the best old-school promoters in the world. He has a way with words and was connected like no one she'd ever met.

She said, "All you need is a bit of publicity and your brand will blow up."

A few weeks later, she told me she'd spoken with him and sent him several of our products. She then says, "he called me last night and said he LOVES your videos and wants to speak with you."

And that's where it started.

With my heart pounding more than it should have, I walked towards the baggage claim and saw several guys in suits all holding up signs. I read through the first five or six, and wondered how this would work. Then, I spot a poster with the name "TRAUTMAN" in large bold print. A short, older Italian gentleman with a fedora, pin-striped suit, and a smile like he was one of the Blues Brothers is behind it.

I smile, point, and say, "Pete?" He grins, extends his hand, and says, "Shawn T R A U T M A A A A N !" in a way that only he could: loudly, proudly, and drawn out on the last name in an impressive manner that garners attention of those around us.

He takes my bag and says, "Come on, we have a lot to do and talk about."

We loaded up into his old-school, lowered black Mercedes-Benz that had to be from the early 80s, and we slow-rolled up and out of the airport like we were about to make a hit.

Traffic was terrible, but Pete navigated the streets like a boss, ignoring the concert of honking horns all around.

We drove in and around Manhattan, Queens, Long Island, the Bronx, and all the little side streets, alleys, and suburbs in between for the next several hours. We drove through with our windows down, coffees in hand, and talked.

I should mention that when I say he was an old-school promoter, I mean it. He told me a lengthy story about when he was Elvis Presley's promoter. And then the Beatles, the Rolling Stones, Bob Dylan, Frank Sinatra, and, of course, The Jackson 5 (to name but a few).

Seriously?

Yep. His name is Pete, and his unofficial tagline is that he made unknowns into stars and stars into superstars. He was also called, "The World's #1 Promotion Man," by Billboard Magazine.

My take on this guy was that he was a storyteller of storytellers. He was a man's man and a go-getter like I'd never met. He was charismatic and full of zest, confidence, and wisdom.

"Here's how promotion works," he said, as we pulled up to an intersection where probably a hundred people were standing and waiting to cross the road.

"THE BEST INSTRUCTOR IN THE WORLD IS RIGHT HERE..." he started. "SHAWN TRAUTMAN! THERE'S NO ONE LIKE HIM. LOOK HIM UP. HE'S THE BEST AND HE'S RIGHT HERE!"

He legit created a buzz out of thin air. "When someone like me believes in you and tells others...people listen," he explained.

Then, he calls his friend Pierce Brosnan. You know, the four-time 007. Pete introduced me to him and said, "Remember his name. He's the BEST instructor in the world." Pierce laughed and welcomed me before Pete wrapped up the call.

From there, Pete asked questions, and I answered with stories. I asked questions and Pete answered with stories. Pete got emotional. I got emotional.

By lunchtime, I'd heard so many stories that blew my mind. Details of back-room deals, contracts of big-name stars that almost didn't happen, and legal battles. And then tales of mistresses, child custody suits, people that went missing, and how it's all part of the entertainment industry. He even shared with me all the companies he'd worked for and how it all changed when he chose to go independent and got to do things his way.

And then, it got interesting.

Pete says he's getting hungry and will take me to a little-known restaurant I've never heard of. We slowly pull up and park behind a few other cars. We then take a short walk and turn down a hidden alley with old brick walls surrounding us. My heart was racing, but I tried not to show it.

Moments later and he's walking ahead of me... and not saying much.

For real, there are times in your life when you have to trust that someone else knows what they're doing and where they're going. This was one of those for me. I trusted him, but I was skeptical.

He slowed, looked carefully at the wall, knocked on a particular brick, and suddenly, the brick slid open. Eyes peered out, then, "Welcome Back, Mr. B!" as the door slid open.

"NO WAY!" I say.

"This is where I go to eat when I don't want to be bothered."

We walk in, the door quickly closes behind us and all of a sudden I'm standing in the middle of a hustling, bustling restaurant with A-listers, B-listers, up-and-coming stars, and a slue of others as he starts nonchalantly telling me who's who as we're walking to our table.

Again, surreal. This whole thing.

At lunch, sixteen people served us. No joke. Sixteen. A new face brought every little thing—napkins, utensils, menu, water, straws, appetizers, etc. Each time someone new came by, he made it a point to introduce me and tell them why it mattered.

An hour later and we're back on the road and talking. Deep, this time. Pete wants to understand my motivations better. Why I do what I do and what drives me. What I want out of life. What matters most to me. How important personal freedoms are.

You know, the basics.

Little did I know, he was sizing me up. He was taking it all in and about to have a real heart-to-heart with me. It was a side of Pete Bennett that most probably never saw. I know this because he told me so.

"I'm going to talk to you like you're my son," he said in a steady but low—almost fatherly tone. "People trade everything for fame—control, family time, their freedom to choose..."

I was listening, intently.

"If you sign with me today, your life will change instantly. But first, a couple of things..."

My eyes were bulging at this point.

"Shawn, you're a thinker. You make calculated decisions. You decide who you support and why. You get to choose what to say and how to say it. Most importantly, you get to choose your free time and be with your family for all the little things. Just by listening to you talk about your kids I know how much they mean to you..."

His tone and mannerisms were different. I could tell there was something more. Something he wasn't saying, but wanted to. And then he did.

"If we do this, you'll no longer be able to come and go as you please. You'll be told where you need to be, when you need to be there, what you're wearing, what you'll say, what you won't say, and who you'll support. In other words, someone else will own you."

I nodded, bit my lip, and was working my way through his comments when he dropped this little nugget.

"To be honest, I'd love to see you become a household name, but I'd be disappointed for you. You only get one chance to raise your kids, to be there for all of life's milestones, and to hold their hand and guide them."

His voice softened, and he continued with glossy eyes.

"I hope you choose to go build something great out of the life you already have. Do it your way. Help people in as many ways as you can, and don't let money be the driving factor in your decisions. Keep building what you're building, and your time will come."

I thanked him for his candid insights about the industry and for sharing so many stories with me. He laughed and told me how he had started writing his autobiography, but it was so much work as it revealed the life he'd lived, all the people he'd worked with, and stories he was a part of along the way.

He said it would be a bestseller, and I had no doubts.

At the time I'd say Pete was in his mid-70s. I kept up with him for a while afterwards and he regularly commented on pictures I'd sent him of family and he always made sure to tell me I made the right decision.

Looking back now, I realize that day with "Pete" was more than a meeting—it was a wake-up call. He helped me see what I couldn't before. That fame isn't the real prize in life—authenticity, freedom, and family are. It was truly a moment that shaped not just my career, but my entire life.

Something else happened that day, too. While riding around in that old Mercedes with Pete, he did more than just promote me—he made me believe in myself. Pete also showed me the power of someone believing in you before you do—a lesson I carry with me as a father.

I had high hopes for his book but later learned that a heart attack prevented it from happening and that he passed as a result.

Mr. Bennett, I'd like to showcase you in mine. Meeting you was a highlight of my life, but getting to know you was even better. Thank you for showing me the power of believing in someone, how honest, genuine promotions work, how to live your life the way you want, and for showing me the authentic version of you when I needed it most.

There's no doubt in my mind that if I'd chosen differently that day, I would have missed out on so many of the memories with my kids like watching them all take their first steps, their first words, singing every day on the way to school, the bike rides, the dance recitals, the games, the tournaments, the awards. All of it.

The right path for each of us is the one that aligns best with our values.

And, here's the fascinating intersection of our lives. Thanks to Pete and our conversation that day, I did it MY WAY, just like Frank Sinatra sang about... when Pete was his promoter. Ironically, "My Way" just so happened to be one of Pete's favorites and something he believed firmly in for his own life.

Thanks for being a part of my story, Pete, and for being my promoter—even if it was just for a day.

MAKING IT MATTER

Essence of the Moment

Staying true to your values, even in the face of life-changing opportunities, leads to a more authentic and fulfilling life. The freedom to live and choose your own path is often the greatest gift you can give to yourself and your loved ones.

Timeless Truths

- ☑ **Authenticity is Priceless:** The most meaningful paths align with your true self, not external expectations or fleeting opportunities.
- ☑ **Family and Freedom Matter Most:** Prioritizing what truly matters—time with loved ones and personal autonomy.
- ☑ **The Power of Saying No:** Turning down opportunities that conflict with your values can be the most empowering decision you make.

Bringing It Home

1. **Clarify Your Priorities:** Write down your top three priorities in life and how they align with your core values. Use this list as a guide when making decisions starting today and throughout the week.
2. **Reach Out with Gratitude:** Identify someone who has inspired or guided you and send them a heartfelt thank-you message. Take the time this week to let them know how their support has shaped your journey.
3. **Encourage Someone's Potential:** Find someone who may doubt their abilities—perhaps a friend, family member, or colleague—and give them genuine encouragement. Aim to do this by the end of the month to make a meaningful impact on their confidence.

Next Level Thinking

Ask yourself:
- ▷ What areas of my life would look different if I fully committed to doing things my way?
- ▷ How do I ensure my decisions reflect my priorities rather than external pressures?
- ▷ What trade-offs am I currently making that might not align with the life I truly want to live?
- ▷ How can I focus on values over validation to ensure I live authentically?

Insight to Remember

"Do it your way. Help people in as many ways as you can, and don't let money be the driving factor in your decisions."
- Pete Bennett

02

THE PRESENT

You don't get too many chances.

Scratch that—I don't get too many chances.

It's seven in the morning, and we're on the road. Just me, my dad, and my son. A "father-son" trip for Father's Day with just the guys as we searched for the perfect present.

We're heading to a place just south of Knoxville, TN, where we have a big day planned. The driving time for the round trip is estimated to be just over six hours.

I'm driving with my dad beside me. We talked for the first twenty minutes, and then I had an idea.

"I have an audiobook I think you'll like, Dad."

Moments later, we're listening to a parable about two little mice and two little people chasing cheese. Cheese, in this story, represents success and change.

We'd listen for about five minutes and then talk for ten. Then listen for five and talk for twelve. And so on.

We talked about our own lives and our own experiences and how spot-on the book was. It nailed it regarding the lessons it presented and how the characters received them.

"Are we close yet?" I hear. "I need to use the little boy's room."

Ha. That was not from my son. The very next exit is where my daughters go to college, but my dad hasn't seen it yet. Perfect! Two birds with one stone.

A quick drive through campus and on to a coffee shop downtown as he's really "gotta go." When we walked with coffee in hand, we saw an old car show that was being set up, and my dad's face lit up.

Old Stingrays, a Model-T, a mint 69 Camaro, some Chevy Novas, and many more. My dad swaps stories with the owners and is beaming with reflectiveness.

"I love just sitting back and watching moments like this," I tell my son. "It's like we're in a time warp, and the world is back to when it was simple."

Back on the road and listening to more parables and talking cheese when we find an old 50's Diner in Sevierville, TN. "Can you believe this place?" my dad exclaims.

The highlight of the stop was when Shannon, our delightfully playful waitress, brought out a Pine Float. My dad had excused himself to use the restroom a few minutes earlier to coordinate with Shannon on what it was.

My dad insisted my son order one, and about two minutes later, it arrived. Not only did it show up, it was accompanied by contagious laughter from the two of them. So much so that my dad had tears in his eyes when he fist-bumped and thanked our server.

Oh, and when my dad was gone, my son leaned over and whispered, "I know which character Grampy is from the book." Later, we'd ask my dad, and he called himself on the same.

We leave, and not five minutes later, we arrive at our destination. A place that touts the label of "The Worlds Largest Knife Store." Does this place disappoint? Not even close.

The next several hours were spent looking in amazement, talking incessantly, and being blown away by what was available. Tasers, swords, knives, guns, and everything in between. We're still going ninety-to-nothing when we hear the message that the store's about to close.

We found the "somewhere" Jimmy Buffett was singing about as five o'clock rolled in like the fog. And we hadn't made any purchases yet—lots of ideas though.

Dang it.

We're nine hours into our journey, and my seventy-eight-year-old dad hasn't lost any steam. Impressive. A quick stop for coffee and gas and now to make the three-hour trip back home and talk some more cheese.

Nope.

Directions have us taking back roads for some reason. A little digging later, and "some reason" is that the interstate is shut down due to a bad wreck. So we reroute.

Beautiful, mind you, but really out in the middle of nowhere. Our three-hour trip home increases to just over four hours, but you know what? We're moving—precisely what we wouldn't have been doing the other way.

A little over two hours in, and we're looking for a bathroom again. Not easy pickings either. We made it to a small town and tried four different places, and each told us they had no public restrooms. We settle in on a McDonald's and quickly take care of business.

Earlier in the day, my dad told me about an old neighbor in Florida who had moved to TN five years ago, but he had no idea where. He meant to call him several times, but we were lost in a maze trying to find our cheese.

Nonetheless, my dad makes the call in this random little town while we're sitting in the parking lot about to leave.

"Timmy!!! This is Bruce!" That's how it started.

Would you believe we were IN the small town where Tim and his lovely wife Rosemary live? Not just that, we were not but five minutes away from them.

"Come on over!"

Minutes later, we're pulling up to both of them standing outside on their porch with the kind of grins you can only see after years of not seeing a treasured friend.

Hugs galore, then food, drinks, and a tour. They're the most welcoming couple I've ever been around, and I'm taking mental notes.

The tour consists mainly of Tim's impressive barn that houses all his toys. We're talking trucks, boats, off-road vehicles, and a wicked cool old jeep that my son just loved.

"Do you want to ride in it? I'll take you down to the mountain real quick."

My dad declines, but my son and I are like, "Heck Yeah!"

He fires it up, and we're off. Lots of vibration due to forty-inch swampers, tons of noise due to the souped-up engine, and a little bit of sliding around due to no seatbelts.

I'm thinking we're going to go see the mountain. You know, like: "There it is, what do you think?"

Yeah, no. It was more like: "Okay, we're here. Hold on."

I've seen this kind of thing before and said, "NO WAY," more times than I can count. We're talking a one-lane rocky road that no car could ever climb. Twisting, turning, bouncing, bumping, sliding—yep, all included for the price of admission.

Ten minutes later, we get to the top. Well, it was one of the lookouts anyway. We look out, absorb the entirety of the landscape while snapping a picture, and then I ask Tim, "How do we get down?"

He laughs childishly and blurts out, "Same way!"

"But it's a one-lane road."

He laughs again and says, "The bigger one usually wins."

And so we start our trek. Going down while bouncing and sliding is a whole lot scarier. Like, there are rock walls close enough for me to reach out my window and touch. Some branches even found their way inside my window and smacked me in the face.

Halfway down, it happens—lights are coming up. People start screaming. They insist on continuing. We have an intense stalemate for about twenty seconds, and then they push forward. Tim gets as tight to the right as he can, with the rock wall now hitting his mirror.

Yep. It's that close.

This other off-road vehicle somehow manages to squeeze its way through without falling off the cliff to its right, and the passengers all start celebrating.

"Has anyone ever fallen off?" I inquire with genuine interest.

"Oh yeah, it happens several times a year..." Then, I lost track of what he was saying because we were now bouncing and sliding our way down the winding rock road.

Just after nine o'clock, we arrived safely back at his house. The tour continues inside, and then we sit, talk, and eat—for hours. Rosemary is absolutely smitten by my son and keeps feeding him. It's the funniest thing ever.

"I've never seen someone eat as much as him...this boy is starving," she says in the most grandmotherly way possible.

At midnight, we say our goodbyes and make plans for a follow-up trip. We still have two hours to go.

My dad is yet to take a break. No naps. No slowing down. No nothing. Well, bathroom breaks, yes. But slowing down? Nope!

One in the morning rolls around, and we manage to make it home. Oh, there was a time change from Eastern to Central on the final two hours. We did, in fact, continue our talks about cheese and the lessons learned from our book (by the way, the book is called *Who Moved My Cheese?* and it's worth hearing).

In retrospect, this wasn't just a trip, it was a rare moment when we had an opportunity to bond—and we took it. Talking, joking, telling stories, thinking deeper about life, seeing old friends, and just enjoying each other's company.

Turns out THAT was the gift. Something that couldn't be bought. The one Father's Day that I can truly say was all about the present.

Being present, that is.

MAKING IT MATTER

Essence of the Moment

Life's most valuable moments are found in the present. Recognizing and cherishing the now allows us to create memories that resonate long after they pass.

Timeless Truths

- ☑ **Presence is a Gift:** The ability to be truly present is both a choice and a treasure that enriches life's most meaningful experiences.
- ☑ **Little Moments Make Great Memories:** The little details—laughter, connection, and shared experiences—make the present unforgettable.
- ☑ **The Power of Togetherness:** Time spent with loved ones creates connections and memories that outlast any material gift.

Bringing It Home

1. **Practice Mindful Connection:** Dedicate ten uninterrupted minutes today to deeply connect with someone you care about. Put away distractions, listen intently, and savor the moment as it unfolds.
2. **Celebrate Shared Time:** Set aside a few hours this week to spend with a loved one doing something simple yet meaningful, like taking a walk, sharing a meal, or reminiscing about cherished memories.
3. **Create a Bonding Experience:** Plan an outing or activity before the month ends that allows you to create new memories with family or friends—a road trip, game night, or visit to a favorite spot.

Next Level Thinking

Ask yourself:
- How would my relationships and experiences change if I fully embraced the power of the present moment?
- What small, meaningful habits can I create to ensure I'm more present daily?
- How can I prioritize spending quality time with loved ones despite a busy schedule?
- What simple traditions or activities can I create to strengthen bonds with the people who matter most?

Insight to Remember

"It wasn't just a trip—it was a rare moment when we had an opportunity to bond—and we took it."

03

A PURPOSEFUL LIFE

The moment he said what he said, it hit me in the feels. He could have given me a thousand reasons why he kept saying no, but none would have landed like this one did.

For three months, I'd been stopping by his place, asking if I could help with everything he had going on.

It had become an ongoing joke for me. I'd call and ask him for help with something, he'd pop right over, no hesitation. Then I'd hear what he was up to and pop over to return the favor—only to get shot down.

Every. Single. Time.

The man was busy. The kind of man who works as if the day had no end, steady and unyielding, fueled by determination and pride in what he does. No complaints, excuses, nor signs of slowing down—even at the age of 80.

He was up at 4am every morning tending to cows, cutting and haying over 90 acres, fixing tractors, welding, and caring for a massive garden—and that's just for starters.

"There's no shortage of work," I'd said to Joanna, throwing my hands up in frustration. "Why won't he let me help?"

"Maybe he just doesn't like working with others?" Joanna quipped with a laugh.

It didn't make sense.

Then, one Saturday morning in June, it happened. He finally told me why. And it wasn't what I thought it would be.

I was there with a friend, walking through his garden. He showed us what was ready to pick and explained how everything worked.

"How about if we stay and get these done for you?" I asked, thinking surely he wouldn't turn me down in front of a guest.

But he did.

He pulled me aside, leaned in close, and began to speak in a tone that told me this was serious.

"You keep asking to help...and I appreciate it," he started, his voice low but steady. "But if you do what you're asking, I won't have any reason to get up in the morning."

I froze.

At first, I thought he was joking, but his face said otherwise.

"When a man loses his purpose, he fades away and dies," he continued. "And I need to know I'm needed and capable—so please don't ask me again."

I blinked. My chest tightened, and my mind scrambled to process what he'd just said.

In that moment, my perspective shifted completely. I saw the situation from a new angle; one I had never even considered before.

He wasn't being stubborn or proud—he was holding on to the one thing that mattered most: his purpose.

As I walked away that day, his words lingered. The more I thought about them, the more profound they became.

Everyone needs a reason to get up in the morning. To feel needed, capable, and purposeful—both for themselves and for the people who depend on them.

I realized then that what I considered "helping" was really closer to "taking."

And what I was asking would have been "taking" something away from him. Something vital.

That realization hit hard. All my life, I've tried to help people—especially older people. My thinking was that it was always the best thing to do.

But sometimes, people need to do things themselves—not because they don't need help, but because they need to feel capable, strong, and whole.

I see now that human dignity is tied to purpose. When we take over for someone struggling, we might ease their burden, but we also risk taking away their reason to keep going.

He taught me that lesson with such clarity that I'll never forget it. A lesson that I get to use regularly—especially with my dad. I occasionally find myself walking away and letting him struggle, just so he knows he's needed and capable.

That day, I walked away with a new understanding of what it means to truly respect someone. I saw, firsthand, the importance of the phrase, "I need to know I'm needed and capable"—and why it matters.

And that, my friends, is a lesson I'll carry with me always: to honor the dignity in purpose and to understand that sometimes, the greatest help we can give is to know when to let someone do what they do and be as they are.

MAKING IT MATTER

Essence of the Moment

Purpose fuels the human spirit. It gives us the drive to rise, the strength to endure, and the dignity to persevere. This story highlights the profound importance of letting others maintain their sense of purpose, even when we're tempted to help.

Timeless Truths

- ☑ **Purpose Preserves Dignity:** Feeling needed and capable is essential for maintaining self-worth and a sense of identity.
- ☑ **Help Can Harm:** Sometimes, stepping in to ease someone's burden unintentionally removes their reason to keep going.
- ☑ **Respect Builds Connection:** Truly understanding and valuing someone's choices fosters trust and strengthens relationships.

Bringing It Home

1. **Recognize the Value of Purpose:** Take time today to observe someone close to you and identify what fuels their sense of purpose. Reflect on how you can respect and support that without taking it over.
2. **Offer, Don't Insist:** When offering help this week, make it clear that you respect their ability to decide. Allow their "no" to stand as a way of honoring their independence and self-worth.
3. **Reframe Your Perspective:** Before the month ends, consciously shift your mindset from "helping" to "honoring" in a specific situation. Focus on the strength and dignity in their efforts rather than trying to ease their struggles.

Next Level Thinking

Ask yourself:
- How often do I "help" without considering what the other person truly needs or wants?
- What could I do differently to empower those around me rather than inadvertently diminish their sense of purpose?
- How can I better distinguish between helping someone and honoring their independence?
- In what ways can I support the people I care about without unintentionally undermining their sense of purpose?

Insight to Remember

"Human dignity is tied to purpose. When we take over for someone who's struggling, we might ease their burden, but we also risk taking away their reason to keep going."

04

BACK TO THAT

The sound of the harmonica pulled me back to that moment. It wasn't just any harmonica—it was *that* harmonica, the one from Clint Black's "State of Mind."

Instantly, I was back at my old nightclub, Neon Moon, watching a lip-sync battle. The dance floor was empty except for one brave soul named John—armed with a muted microphone. John owned the space as he mouthed every word and performed in a way only he could. The crowd was electric, the moment—unforgettable.

It's funny how music can do that—how a melody can unlock a memory, transporting us back to that moment in time we thought we'd left behind. No warning, no nothing—just instantaneous snapshots in our minds that are as real as they were the first time.

Songs aren't just notes and words—they're like time machines, cued up and waiting for the right moment to carry us back.

Take, for instance, the day I got a call from my friend Kim. My Grandpa Wally had just passed unexpectedly after surgery in the hospital where she was working. Her words hit me like a freight train. Numbly, I turned the radio on while sitting in the Best Buy parking lot. I was searching for something—anything. The first song I heard was Sarah McLachlan's "Angel." Lyrics that felt like they were written for that moment filled the airwaves, "In the arms of the angel, fly away from here." Even now, that song takes me back to that parking lot and steals my breath.

For years, "My Girl" by the Temptations was my daughters' bedtime anthem. Every night, I'd stand them on my feet, hold them tight while I spun them around, and sing those familiar lines, "I've got sunshiiiine on a cloudy day..." Their giggles would echo through the room. Even now, when we hear that song, I see their tiny feet on mine, their faces lighting up in that special way only a child's can.

"Little Sister" by Dwight Yoakam just happens to be the first song I ever choreographed a dance routine for—and it was for a brother/sister duo named Dani and Colby. I can't hear that song without returning to that event and seeing their big smiles and little country outfits while they performed.

"Springsteen" by Eric Church is another that holds a special place. It was the soundtrack to countless car rides to school. My youngest, just barely able to form complete sentences, would belt out the chorus in her tiny, sweet voice. I still get a lump in my throat every time I hear it.

"Rainbow" by Kacey Musgraves takes me back to that middle school auditorium during the Talent Show. I'm in the back row, and my daughter, Breanna, is on the stage. The nerves, anticipation, and excitement were all fluttering around inside of me until she started singing. Within seconds, it all disappeared as she belted out her heartfelt rendition of the song that stunned the crowd and left people talking for months.

Then there's "Chicken Fried" by the Zac Brown Band. One note, and I'm back at the Round-Up, a saloon-style country bar in Tampa. I'm two-stepping with my friends Jen and Ted, the smell of sawdust on the floor and the clinking of beer bottles filling the air. It's not just a memory—it's a feeling—the kind of freedom and fun you don't fully appreciate until it's gone.

Not all songs are tied to places, though. Some are tied to people.

"The Devil Went Down to Georgia" will forever belong to my good friend, Mark. I'll never forget him dancing to it like no one was watching on his wedding night. He put on a show and made everyone laugh. That moment and that song are now bittersweet reminders of him, and every time I hear it, I go back to that venue and watch it again—for the first time.

And I can't forget the night of our wedding. Jim Brickman's "Love of My Life" started playing, and the world seemed to pause alongside our first dance. Just hearing the first couple of piano keys takes me back to that moment with all my friends and family watching. I can still see Steve and Patty, John and Dr. Nancy, Chris and Courtney, Dennis, Adam, William, Nicki, Andrea, Bonnie, Kurt, and so many others—all like it was yesterday.

I probably have a hundred or more songs that instantly bring me back to that one thing—whatever that one thing was. And that's the power of music—it's a keeper of moments. It's a bridge to memories we didn't realize were waiting for us.

The beauty of it all is that music doesn't just bring back memories; it brings back feelings—raw, unfiltered, and real. It can make us smile, cry, or laugh out loud. The right song can turn an ordinary day into something extraordinary and a fleeting moment into one we'll cherish forever.

As for you—think about the songs that stop you in your tracks. Which ones take you back to that one moment that shaped you, the people who mattered, and the memories that linger? Share them with others. Relive them in your mind. People need to see what you have stored up in that mind of yours.

Because sometimes, the soundtrack to our lives is the key to remembering what makes life so profoundly beautiful.

MAKING IT MATTER

Essence of the Moment

Music is more than sound. It holds our memories and emotions, reconnecting us to moments we thought were long gone. It transforms fleeting experiences into timeless treasures, reminding us of the beauty in our lives.

Timeless Truths

- ☑ **Music Bridges Time:** A single melody can transport us to a place, person, or emotion from our past with vivid clarity.
- ☑ **Feelings Resurface:** The right song doesn't just bring back a memory—it revives the emotions tied to it, reminding us of who we were and what mattered most.
- ☑ **Songs Deepen Connection:** Sharing the stories behind the songs we love strengthens bonds and keeps memories alive across generations.

Bringing It Home

1. **Curate Your Soundtrack:** When you find yourself with a quiet moment today, create a playlist of songs that hold deep meaning for you. Let it become a personal time machine to revisit cherished memories and reflect on what shaped you.
2. **Share the Stories Behind the Songs:** The next time a meaningful song plays, take the opportunity to share the story it brings to life with someone close to you. Use it as a way to connect and inspire them to reflect on their own memories.
3. **Be Present with the Music:** Set aside an evening this month to listen to your playlist without distractions. Allow the music to take you back to the emotions and moments it carries, reconnecting you to what truly matters.

Next Level Thinking

Ask yourself:
- What songs hold the most meaning for me, and why?
- How can I use music to reconnect with people, memories, or moments that shaped who I am?
- What steps can I take to preserve and share the stories tied to the songs that matter most?
- How can I use music to celebrate the moments and relationships that have shaped me?

Insight to Remember

"Sometimes, the soundtrack to our lives is the key to remembering what makes life so profoundly beautiful."

05

MO MONEY

For six weeks, it remained untouched. Water, mud, sand, mold, dirt, insulation, and sweat were all regulars. Cold showers were a thing, but they were fast.

My son and I had just worked in some of the most horrendous conditions on Ft. Myers Beach in FL. It was all related to Hurricane Ian and we were exhausted from twelve to fourteen-hour days, once for fifteen days straight.

Twelve years earlier, my son was getting his first-ever haircut. He laughed, cried, and did everything in between. I have pictures of that day and remember it like it was yesterday. The guy who cut his hair was named Mo.

Mo, short for Morris, was one of my all-time favorite barbers. He was great at what he did, asked lots of questions, and told wonderful stories. The kind of stories you could only get "at the barbershop."

When I first met Morris, it was an accident. The guy I was there to see had to leave, and Morris just happened to be available and welcomed me to his chair. That was all it took. Instant connection and he became my go-to barber.

As fate would have it, we moved out of the area some five years earlier and hadn't seen Mo in years, though we kept in touch online. As we were on our way home for Thanksgiving, I thought I'd give him a shout to see if he was still in the business.

Turns out, he was. He had opened a place in Dunedin, FL, called McGuire's Barber Shop and was living his dream. We asked If he had any openings as we were just passing through and had six weeks' worth of hair growth. Mo excitedly said, "No, but I'll stay late for you guys if you can be here by 5:30."

That afternoon, we got caught in traffic, rerouted several times, and eventually found ourselves nearly thirty minutes late. We had kept Mo informed, and he told us to keep going and be safe and that he'd wait for us.

We sat and talked with Mo for well over an hour about our last six weeks. The forty-thousand dollars cash we found for one of the homeowners. The purple heart collection that was buried in over three feet of mud. The trailer full of heavy equipment that fishtailed on me and somehow didn't flip while on the interstate.

And the stories of heartbreak. The folks that lost everything. The tales of finding their neighbors in the canals. The horror stories of those who stayed and endured the storm surge. The people who were still missing.

Mo asked question after question and was genuinely interested. He showed compassion and empathy throughout the talk and had to stop cutting several times to regroup as we could see he was emotional. He was sad that his American brothers and sisters, just a few hours down the road, had to endure what they did and that he couldn't do anything for them.

Then, with tears in his eyes, he thanked us for what we had done and for sharing it with him in such a personal way that mattered.

He then informed us that payment for our haircuts had already been made. The currency was the stories of what we'd just lived—that they were worth much more to him than money, and that we paid our dues.

He called it "Mo Money" and said it was the best possible payment one could make.

You see, very few times in my life have I witnessed the kind of connection I saw during those six weeks. People were just people. Looking out for one another. Providing basic needs. There were no agendas, no political divides, no race-baiting. Just people from all ages and stages walking, talking, hugging, supporting, and loving one another.

Mo gets it. Mo cares. Mo knows what's important in this world, and it sure isn't money. Most admirably, Mo values his community and its people more than anything.

So, yeah, Mo is much mo' than just a barber—he's a role-model... to all of us. Pay attention to the little things, be a great conversationalist, give back where you can, and treat others with dignity. For humanity's sake, it all matters.

MAKING IT MATTER

Essence of the Moment

True wealth isn't measured in money but in the connections we build and the compassion we show. Mo's heartfelt gratitude and sense of community remind us that the most meaningful exchanges are often priceless.

Timeless Truths

- ☑ **Conversations Carry Weight:** Open, heartfelt exchanges can turn ordinary moments into deeply meaningful connections.
- ☑ **Empathy Makes a Difference:** Genuine interest and compassion can transform everyday interactions into profound connections.
- ☑ **Kindness Strengthen Bonds:** Even simple acts of kindness, like staying late or listening deeply, can leave a lasting impression and strengthen community bonds.

Bringing It Home

1. **Value Conversations:** The next time someone shares a personal story, take a moment to truly listen without distractions. Like Mo, ask thoughtful questions and show

genuine empathy—it's often in these exchanges that deeper connections are made.

2. **Show Gratitude:** Think about someone who has gone above and beyond for you, as Mo did by staying late and showing heartfelt care. This week, express your thanks in a meaningful way, whether through a sincere conversation, a note, or a small act of kindness.

3. **Support Someone in Need:** Look for someone in your community who might need a hand or a moment of compassion. Take a step, as Mo did in offering his time and understanding, to provide meaningful support without expecting anything in return.

Next Level Thinking

Ask yourself:
- When was the last time I truly listened to someone's story without distractions?
- How can I prioritize compassion and connection in my everyday encounters?
- How can I make someone feel truly seen and valued through a small gesture or act of kindness?
- In what ways can I prioritize meaningful connections over transactional interactions in my daily life?

Insight to Remember

"Payment for our haircuts had already been made. The currency was the stories of what we'd just lived—that they were worth much more to him than money, and that we paid our dues."

06

ONE DAY AT A TIME

W hen I first met Don, he carried himself like someone who had life dialed in. Little did I know his story would redefine how I see resilience and recovery.
And what a breath of fresh air this guy was.

Don was the IT guy for the entire floor of Gov't employees and contractors, where I had just accepted my new assignment. We hit it off immediately, and he became my go-to, not just for IT-related issues, but for life advice, as he was thirteen years my elder and seemed to have it all together.

Over the past twenty years, Don and I have shared countless conversations that deepened our connection. After leaving Gov't contract work, Don and I stayed in touch via phone and social media. His ability to synthesize information, make sense of it, and share his thoughts in ways that help humanity is second to none.

He's smart, intelligent, witty, and quirky. He laughs at himself, tells people how much he appreciates them and speaks up for the disadvantaged in ways most never consider.

But there was something more. Something I didn't know about him, and when I discovered it—it shook me to the core.

He commented to someone about a talk he'd given in 2014 and said he had it recorded if anyone wanted to hear it. I had free time that day and asked him to send it over. He said, "I'll pull it up and send it, but don't feel obligated to listen."

41

Of course, that was code for, "There's something here worth hearing if you're daring enough to listen."

I saw that it was forty minutes, cringed, and went and poured a cup of coffee. I figured it was just him talking about his life and what all brought him to where he is. Wrong!

It was a talk that grabbed me, pulled me in, and then punched me in the gut over and over until it ended. I was physically and mentally exhausted when it finished, as it was so real and relatable.

Simply stated, Don's story is a testament to the resilience of the human spirit and the power of community and discipline in overcoming life's darkest challenges. His story is also about legacy and what we leave behind for others.

In other words—it was his life story—before I knew who he had become.

The recording was at an AA meeting where Don had been asked to speak. It was right around his 20th anniversary of being sober. Though he wanted to prepare for the talk, he felt it best to be "in the moment" and talk from the heart.

Authenticity tends to capture attention. From the moment he started speaking, "My sobriety date is March 17th, 1994—St. Patty's Day," to the closing line of, "Thank you for listening," I was hooked.

In forty minutes flat, Don walked through his childhood, his mental obsessions, and alcoholism in a way that is gripping, realistic, and eye-opening. He shared how alcohol led him to self-destructive behaviors, strained relationships, and suicidal thoughts.

He was empty and unfulfilled, no matter what he did.

Don then describes, in breathtaking detail, many near-death experiences, including failed suicide attempts, and what it took for him to realize the severity of his addiction and why it necessitated change.

Past that, he shared what the fellowship of Alcoholics Anonymous (AA) did for him and how it provided a sense of belonging and accountability. Service to others, even in small ways, became a cornerstone of his recovery.

What he'd learned from a broken life has gone on to help so many others—because he's earned the right to share what worked for him and not try to tell anyone else what they should do. Letting go of his ego is but one of many mindset hacks he's used to help him grow and avoid relapses.

"I don't know what I don't know" is one such story he tells. It's how he often has to question his own mind about what is happening around him. How he doesn't know what anyone else is really going through or where they've been. And how it helps him to disconnect from feelings—as they aren't facts.

But that's not where it ended for me. Not only did I listen to Don's talk multiple times, but I've now shared it with dozens of people who needed to hear it and had follow-up talks as it relates.

The talk itself is powerful, but knowing Don and seeing who he is today helps me use his testimony as a bridge to help others and to provide a perspective on the world that very few can give.

For me, big takeaways from his talk include thoughts like these: recovery is a process, not a destination. Personal accountability is key. Small acts of discipline and service build important foundations. Changing one's mindset is essential for overcoming addiction. Being present matters. Spirituality and connection are critical elements of healing.

And then there's this: one day at a time. Give us *this* day our daily bread—not tomorrow's. We have to do what we need to do today. A thousand times a day we have to choose what's right for us—not just once. Yesterday doesn't matter—what matters is today—right now.

With that, we never know how our actions today will affect someone else tomorrow, but we have to show up and try. What Don did that day was courageous in and of itself, but it extended far beyond that room. He left a detailed account of something so personal, yet profound—and did so in a way that could help others for years to come.

I often talk about legacy and how what we do today matters for what we leave behind—but it's not usually clouded in darkness. Don's talk, however, reminds us that sharing our vulnerabilities is not just brave—it's a lifeline for others. Stories of rock-bottom moments connect with our souls in ways most can't, and they illuminate paths of hope for those still struggling.

I'm grateful for Don, not just for who he is now, but for the courage it took to leave his old self behind. His journey proves why we must never give up on ourselves or those we love.

And I'll close this chapter with a tagline he uses regularly that sums up who he is today. A line that is both a prayer and a call to action—inspiring kindness, mindfulness, and a commitment to alleviating the pain and challenges faced by most humans and animals:

"May all Sentient Beings Be Released From Suffering."

MAKING IT MATTER

Essence of the Moment

Don's story underscores the resilience of the human spirit, showing how vulnerability and dedication to change can lead to profound transformation. It's a powerful reminder that recovery, legacy, and service to others are built one day at a time.

Timeless Truths

- ☑ **Vulnerability Connects Us:** Sharing your struggles can bridge gaps and create opportunities for healing—for yourself and others.
- ☑ **Recovery is a Journey:** True healing requires daily effort, personal accountability, and small, consistent steps forward.
- ☑ **Courage Inspires Change:** Facing and sharing our vulnerabilities can spark transformation—not just within ourselves, but in others who witness our journey.

Bringing It Home

1. **Reflect on Your Legacy:** Take a quiet moment to think about how you want to be remembered. Write down one way you can start living that legacy today, inspired by Don's courage and authenticity.
2. **Be of Service:** Find a simple way to support someone around you this week, just as Don discovered in his recovery. Whether it's offering a kind word, being a listening ear, or sharing your own story, focus on how your actions might create a ripple effect.
3. **Take It One Day at a Time:** Challenge yourself this month to approach each day with mindfulness and intention. Let go of yesterday's worries and focus on making decisions that align with your values, moment by moment.

Next Level Thinking

Ask yourself:
▷ How does service to others help shape my sense of purpose?
▷ What small steps can I take today to move closer to the life I envision for myself and those I love?
▷ How can I embrace vulnerability to create deeper connections with others and foster healing?
▷ What daily habits or practices can I implement to build a stronger foundation for personal growth and resilience?

Insight to Remember

"One day at a time. Give us this day our daily bread—not tomorrow's. We have to do what we need to do today."

07

SHARING THE SPOTLIGHT

We had no idea how our night would go when we first walked in and heard her. Moments later, we'd welcome the lady singing to our table as she was on a break. What happened next changed a young lady in the most beautiful way.

It all started on a dreary Friday night. Our friend invited me, my son, and my youngest, Kelbie, to dinner. A few of my friend's friends were at a local restaurant where they had live music on the patio. And that's where this story takes place.

It was raining, so we improvised and made a table for twelve by borrowing two nearby tables and chairs. It was crowded, but folks were generous, and before long, we were enamored with "Brian and Bella," the duo who entertained us all in the best possible way.

Brian is an amazing guitarist and he's pretty impressive on the vocals as well. Bella, however, has her own star appeal and vocal ability; together, they make quite the team.

Great food, strong drinks, and lively conversation—all with great background music that was more of a show. The first break comes and that's when we meet Bella in person. "G'day, Mate!" she said in the most unmistakable Australian accent you could imagine.

Bella ends up taking a seat next to my daughter, who takes a liking to her—and vice versa. I complimented Bella on what I'd been hearing and attempted to say, "You sound like it should have." It was my condensed way of saying it was as good as the originals.

"Did you say I sound like a tuna?" she asks with the most inquisitive face you could imagine from across the table, with her mouth slightly open as if to say, "Huh?"

I looked at her—she looked at me. I processed what she said while thinking about what I had said and then responded with how I felt would best solve the situation.

"Yes. Yes I did!" with my head nodding in the affirmative, and a smile that wouldn't let me show any teeth as I tried not to laugh.

The break lasted just over fifteen minutes, and my daughter talked with Bella for most of it. Then, Bella got back on stage and belted out another hour's worth as the crowd just ate it up. Not only is Bella a talented singer, but she's a solid performer and lights up the room in a truly magical way.

On the next break, Bella made time to greet several regulars and thank them for coming out. She did what she does best in that she made everyone feel like they mattered. Then she sat back down and started laughing and telling stories with Kelbie again.

About the time she's to go back on stage, she leans over and says something to the then thirteen-year-old Kelbie that caused Kelbie's eyes to bulge. This, after hearing all about how Kelbie loves to sing and has a beautiful voice. Brian is already out there playing and he's wrapping up a song and expecting Bella to join him.

Instead, Bella grabs Kelbie by the hand, leads her up to the stage and has a quick word with Brian. Kelbie turns and looks at me with a big grin and a total look of excitement bundled with nerves and then Brian's announcement:

"Ladies and gentlemen, let's give Kelbie a round of applause for her debut. She'll be singing Jolene for us tonight."

Bella came back to the table and was just giddy. Her excitement was contagious, and she started cheering Kelbie on to get others to chime in—and they did.

For the first thirty seconds or so, Kelbie's voice was soft. The microphone was too far away, and she hadn't really connected quite yet. Bella motioned to her and told her what to do, and she quickly adjusted.

And from that moment on, Kelbie lit up and stole the show.

At the end—a standing ovation from a crowd of strangers led by a new friend who made it all happen. It was one song, but one song was all it took to make the moment magical.

"Oh my gosh, that was so much fun, thank you!" she said, just dripping with excitement as she returned to the table. "How did I sound?"

Bella took the time to praise Kelbie in the best way possible—all good things. She told her how well she had done and made her feel great about her experience. Bella got back on that stage, but not without leaving an impression on a young lady who had no idea her night would turn out the way it did.

To this day, I hold a special memory and a unique story of how a lady named Bella did something amazing for my daughter—just because she could. It gave me such joy to watch them sit, talk, and connect in ways that only ladies can and to truly support one another by building each other up.

It was needed—both for Kelbie and me. Probably for Bella, too, as she was still reeling from the "tuna" comment that never happened.

Bella's not just a singer and performer—she's a magician. I saw her make something appear out of thin air, and it was just beautiful. Moments like this don't come along often, but when they do, you have to watch them play out.

More importantly—what Bella did that night wasn't just encourage my daughter—she got her to believe in herself. And Bella didn't just talk about it; she made it happen—she physically walked her up there and handed her the mic.

Friends, if you ever get the chance to see or meet her in person, please do. Her name is Bella Jane Astridge, and you can find her on Facebook and Instagram—give her a follow. Thank her at least once for me—and once for Kelbie—and mention that she sounds like a tuna: she loves that!

MAKING IT MATTER

Essence of the Moment

A simple act of encouragement can ignite confidence in someone else, creating memories and connections that last a lifetime. Bella's generosity and Kelbie's bravery turned an ordinary night into an extraordinary moment of shared joy.

Timeless Truths

- ☑ **Encouragement Ignites Bravery:** A little push from someone else can help us uncover courage we didn't know we had.
- ☑ **Kindness Creates Ripples:** The impact of uplifting someone else can echo far beyond the moment, leaving a lasting impression.
- ☑ **Courage is Contagious:** Bravery inspires others to step out of their comfort zones and discover their own potential.

Bringing It Home

1. **Step Into the Spotlight:** If there's something you've been hesitant to try, take a small step toward it today. Whether it's singing, speaking, or sharing your talent, let Kelbie's bravery inspire you to embrace the moment.
2. **Find Someone to Uplift:** Think of someone who could use a boost of confidence or encouragement, like Kelbie did. This week, make a thoughtful gesture—whether it's sharing a kind word, giving them a new opportunity, or simply being present to support them.
3. **Celebrate Others' Wins:** The next time someone achieves something meaningful like Kelbie did with her performance, take the time to acknowledge their success. Cheer them on and show genuine excitement for what they've accomplished the way Bella did—it could mean more than you know.

Next Level Thinking

Ask yourself:

▷ Who could benefit from a boost of confidence, and how can I offer that?
▷ When opportunities arise, will I step out of my comfort zone to create meaningful experiences?
▷ How can I create opportunities for others to shine and build their confidence?
▷ What moments in my life might benefit from a little courage and a willingness to take the first step?

Insight to Remember

"Bella didn't just talk about it, she made it happen—she physically walked her up there and handed her the mic."

08

THANKS FOR GIVING

A series of random circumstances led me to the light just as it turned red. A week before Thanksgiving, I was rushing around, gathering food for our annual dinner—one everyone's already drooling over.

I glanced at my phone and opened Facebook. The very first post I read hit me like a ton of bricks. It was simple, yet profound, and I was lost in thought before I knew it.

I read it again. And again.

The sound of horns blaring behind me jolted me back to reality. The light had turned green, and I was holding up the line. But by then, my mind had already changed—my thoughts were different, and my plans had already shifted.

And somewhere in the middle of it all, I found myself grinning like a Cheshire cat.

That evening, at dinner, I shared my revelation knowing that I'd be met with resistance—MAJOR resistance. "I'd like to postpone our Thanksgiving dinner until Friday," I started, with my words dropping into the silence like stones in water. "I want to help serve meals for those who don't have any."

For a moment, you could hear a pin drop. Six faces stared at me across the table, seemingly unblinking. I wasn't sure if it was shock or outright rejection. I held my breath.

Then, my second eldest broke the silence. "I love that idea!" she said, her voice brimming with excitement.

"That would be awesome," another blurted out, almost simultaneously.

Joanna's face softened with a smile I don't see often enough. "Yay!" she started. "I've always wanted to do something like that!"

Heads nodded all around in agreement—zero resistance.

I sat there, stunned. Total buy-in. At that moment, I realized how much this could mean—not just for me but for all of us.

Thanksgiving morning arrived, and with it, the usual flurry of questions. "What do we wear?" "What will we do?" "How many people will be there?" "How long can we stay?"

I didn't have any of the answers, but it didn't matter. What mattered was that we were going, no matter what.

We arrived an hour before the event was set to open, and we were greeted with the kind of down-home welcome that confirmed we were in the right place. Terry Branscum, the host, came out to meet us with a grin that could light up a room.

"Thank you so much for coming!" he said, his voice warm and grateful. He gave us a quick tour, pointed out where everything was set up, and explained the flow of the day.

This was the eighth year Terry had organized his annual Thanksgiving meal for the community, and it was nothing short of incredible. His post that day on Facebook about needing volunteers changed everything for us—and we were all smiling and taking it in.

Terry's humility was evident. Alongside a Leukemia diagnosis in 2017, he had turned his gratitude for life into action, providing meals, hope, and support for thousands of people over the years. And he wasn't just feeding people—he was creating a space where they felt seen, cared for, and valued.

We jumped into the assembly line without hesitation. Turkey, mashed potatoes, green beans, dessert—it was a well-oiled machine. Behind the walls, volunteers worked the stoves while others served, packed, and handed out meals. Some were even delivering the meals, loading up cars with bags full of meals destined for the community.

We packaged and distributed over 500 hot meals in just a few hours. But it wasn't just about the food. It was the faces. The genuine smiles. The heartfelt thank-you. And the occasional tear of gratitude. I'll never forget the older gentleman who shook my hand

and said, "Happy Thanksgiving!" and then, "You don't know how much this means to me."

By the end of the day, we were physically exhausted but emotionally full. My entire life, I've merely been on the consuming end of Thanksgiving. This was the first time it was about giving. And it changed me.

Receiving "thanks" for "giving" hit me in the best possible way. It reshaped how I saw the holiday—not as a day to simply gorge on food, but as a day to give back to others and to be grateful for what I have.

Terry does so much more than provide meals—he provides hope. He and his team have delivered some 17,000 meals and counting, not just on Thanksgiving but also at Christmas, where gifts are added to the mix. His impact ripples through his community in ways most of us can only imagine.

They say the Lord works in mysterious ways. Well, that post on Facebook—its timing and the fact that it was the only thing I read that day—all aligned to change lives. Mine, my family's, the other volunteers', and the recipients'.

The next night at our Thanksgiving dinner, we all took turns talking about what we were thankful for. I was last to speak, and my answer was, "People like Terry that are out there putting others first and making a difference to so many people in their communities."

And what really hit me was this: it wasn't just about showing up—it was about stepping in, connecting, and being a part of something that truly mattered.

This wasn't just a Thanksgiving to remember—it was a Thanksgiving that transformed us all... all thanks to a guy named Terry, who makes the impossible seem possible through God, love, and action.

MAKING IT MATTER

Essence of the Moment

What started as a rushed errand and a red light became a spark that transformed Thanksgiving into something far more meaningful. By stepping out of our comfort zone to give, we found a deeper connection to gratitude and each other.

Timeless Truths

- ☑ **Little Acts, Huge Impact:** A single decision can create a ripple of change that touches countless lives.
- ☑ **Gratitude Comes Through Giving:** True thankfulness is realized in moments of service and connection.
- ☑ **Communities Need Everyday Heroes:** People like Terry show that one person's efforts can uplift an entire community.

Bringing It Home

1. **Reimagine Thanksgiving:** Plan a Thanksgiving activity centered on helping others, whether it's volunteering, donating, or inviting someone who might otherwise be alone.
2. **Cultivate Conversations of Gratitude:** During your holiday meal, encourage everyone to share a specific person or event they are thankful for this year.
3. **Recognize Everyday Heroes:** Take time to appreciate and thank those in your community, like Terry, who dedicate themselves to improving the lives of others.

Next Level Thinking

Ask yourself:

- How has your understanding of gratitude changed through acts of giving?
- What traditions or habits in your life could shift to include more meaningful contributions to others?
- Who in your community inspires you through their selfless acts, and how can you support or emulate them?
- How might serving others as a family create stronger bonds and shared purpose?

Insight to Remember

"Receiving 'thanks' for 'giving' hit me in the best possible way. It reshaped how I saw the holiday—not as a day to simply gorge on food, but as a day to give back to others."

09

LEGACY

For the last couple of weeks, I thought I had a solid plan—but now, out of the blue, it was unraveling.

To put it mildly, we were out of options.

There was a sinking feeling in my gut, like having a one-shot lead on the eighteenth hole in the Masters, missing the green, and watching your ball trickle towards the water on a steep slope.

We planned to book a flight for the weekend or Monday and send her home. It was Friday, and the first golf tournament of her Freshman year of high school was four days away—on Tuesday.

The largest IT outage in American history occurred that morning; all flights were canceled and nothing could be booked. By late Friday afternoon, we decided it was best just to rent a car and make the twelve-hour drive instead.

Three weeks.

That was the earliest availability we could find due to so many canceled flights. At four o'clock, I felt like the universe was stacking the deck against us.

I check again at six o'clock. Five weeks.

There's an unwritten rule that parents are supposed to make things right. You know, to fix things when they go wrong. Well, here I am, helpless in a situation beyond my control, letting her down in what was supposed to be a defining moment.

What's the real problem? We rented a car to come to FL six weeks prior and have been borrowing a friend's vehicle ever since.

My daughter literally had no way to get home.

At dinner we sat and pondered. We talked about what this might mean for the three of us. What missing the tournament would mean for my youngest. How her team would respond, as they couldn't qualify without her. What missing my second eldest's last couple of weeks before she heads to college would mean. And where we would stay while we wait.

"I'd like to speak to you privately, for a moment."

Those very words are how my next day started. It was now Saturday morning, and the other two were just rolling out of bed. I excused myself and went out back with the guy we were staying with.

We had this guy's garage filled with recently purchased tools as my son was building a pressure washing and landscaping business, and we were helping him. We also had seven properties waiting for us to start as we'd been spending time lining up new work.

This matters more in a moment.

I walk back in, and my kids both see the look on my face. The kind of look where they know something's up. "Is everything okay?" one of them quips.

"Is it okay if I speak with them for a moment?" my friend asks.

I obliged, and they had the same look within about five minutes. My friend then hugs me and heads out for a bike ride, lunch plans, and a Styx concert later that night.

We now had a potential option.

Arrangements had been made for us to receive the keys to a car we could take possession of that afternoon. One we were told had several problems, but that if we could make it work, it would be ours.

He said, "If anyone can turn this car into something usable, it's you guys."

Accepting the keys felt like stepping into the unknown with nothing but a hope and a prayer. Sure, there were voices quietly whispering everything that could go wrong, but louder ones said to have a little faith and give it a shot.

Now, the mad scramble.

Seven hours. That's what we had to wrap everything up. That included the jobs we were working on, returning items that could be returned, going to pawn shops for those that couldn't, and doing our best to refocus our attention.

No time to kill.

Five o'clock rolls around, and we're handed the keys. Within about fifteen minutes, we're at the O'Reillys in Dunedin, FL. I tell the two guys there what just happened and show them what we were given. They immediately light up at how awesome it was that someone would do that for someone else.

Are the tires good? No. They're worn, have gashes in the side of them, and low. They're holding air, so there's that. How's the oil? Very low. Doesn't even read. We add enough oil to make it acceptable and no longer below the line. How 'bout the temp? Running hot—after just five minutes. No coolant at all. We fill that up and hope there are no leaks.

Surely, that's all. Right?

Nope. Check engine light's on. We find two more 'fixable' things. One's the gas cap, and the other removes one code from the check engine warning. What else? Brake light is flashing. We find that the emergency brake is severed and unusable. Windshield wiper fluid box and line is broken so that's out. Windshield wipers are falling apart so we replace them. Front shocks seem to be shot. Radio works.

"You're not really going to drive this all the way up there, are you?"

Over the next couple of hours, I heard different versions of that same question. Each time I answered, it was in the affirmative —that "we'll just start driving and do the best we can." One of the guys even told me he would make it a point to pray for us.

Then, the other said, "Too many things can go wrong. You need to get it all fixed."

"If we wait until everything's perfect, everything won't be perfect. If we take the chance, we've got a chance!" I say with a smile while cringing.

"Okay, but you have to promise to call and let us know how your drive is going. We're both working tomorrow, and we'll be rooting for you!" I agree. Then, I gave them both fist-bumps and thanked them for their time, advice, and concern.

We test drive it to see what the shaking's all about. Turns out it goes away after about forty miles an hour. Cool. I'll just drive faster than that.

Wait, let me back up for a moment. Two strangers who owed me nothing just treated my situation like it mattered. They walked with me, talked with me, looked things up for me, and chose to pray for me.

Think about how great it would be if everyone did that for strangers.

Okay, back to it.

It's now after eight o'clock, the sun is going down, and we've got to gas it up and clean it. Nine o'clock, and we're heading back to my friend's house to start packing. Eleven-thirty comes, and we're finishing the tie-downs on the roof and ready to take a nap.

A quick check of all our fluids at four in the morning and, surprisingly, we're ready to roll—twelve hours to go if our leap of faith pans out.

The first hour and a half in, and we're some eighty miles away. For FL, that's good. Then, an abrupt stop. Not just me, everyone. We're on I-75 northbound when everything comes to a screeching halt.

I can see something about eight cars in front of me that looks like it's on fire. I turn the car off to ensure it doesn't overheat, and we get out and start walking towards the smoke.

Not good.

We see a car off to our left, all mangled and in the median. To our right, another car banged up and partially on the shoulder. A debris field of car parts is littered for about two hundred yards as we start walking up on a third vehicle, partially ripped apart and on the guardrail.

Then, sirens. Police. Ambulances. State Police. Fire Trucks. They all start showing up.

For the next two and a half hours I spoke with different folks standing around on the interstate. I went from car to car and met a wide variety of people. A family from Miami who had been driving since two that morning. Another is on their way to GA. Then, another who had rented a U-Haul and was in the process of helping another family move.

Conversation after conversation, we all laughed and enjoyed swapping stories. It relieved the stress and minimized the tension. And in that moment, surrounded by strangers who were now friends, I realized how shared struggles can break down barriers. We weren't just drivers stuck on an interstate, but fellow humans finding connection in the chaos.

It was pretty cool.

I even got to a point where I was introducing people to others based on similarities. "Bob, you've got to meet this family over here. They're going to the same place you are in GA. Maybe your company could use their company since you both are in the same industry."

You know, things like that.

Before long, we're back at it, and the shaking commences. It seems worse but goes away as we go faster. Another couple of hours go by and we're in GA. Off to a good start. Tires are holding air. Engine's holding oil. Radiator's holding coolant.

Mind you, my check engine light's on, the word "BRAKE" is flashing, the TPMS light is on, and something's smoking from the engine, but we don't know what.

Gotta keep moving.

The way I see it is this. If I can get within three hundred miles of home and something happens, AAA will get me the rest of the way. Only another two hundred or so miles to go before I get to that point.

We're now eight hours into our day and have a good eight hours left. Not where we wanted to be, but we'd had a few extra stops to make sure everything was good (and, of course, we had that accident to wait through).

I call my guys from O'Reilly's and let them know our progress. "That's fantastic!" one of them states. Then, he tells me to hang on so he can tell the other guy. We hear their conversation, and the other guy erupts into a celebration of sorts. He says he was excited that I called to let him know and that he'd been praying for us.

How cool is that? Perfect strangers the night before who took an interest in our story and my family and that they not only helped but also prayed for us.

Then, there is a loud snapping sound from the front left wheel as we leave a Buc-ees. The sound jolts me out of focus, and my heart starts pounding like there's no tomorrow. Panic sets in, and I grip the steering wheel tight.

"WHAT was THAT?"

I'm imagining all sorts of worst-case scenarios, but the car keeps moving, and nothing seems to have happened. I had about a half-mile to go before I had to merge, so I listened intently as I slowly sped up, and sure enough, there were no other sounds.

Gotta keep moving.

We're now limping along with pops, shaking, flashing lights, and a bit of smoke, but we're getting closer. And we're now within the three-hundred-mile range to get us home. Awesome!

Mind you, we had no plan just the day before, and this was somehow better.

An hour to go, and I'm still in drive with a big ole smile on my face. The only new thing is that the steering wheel is now shaking, and when I talk, it sounds like someone is grabbing the skin outside my throat. The kids are amused.

I call O'Reillys one last time, as I know they're getting ready to close, and I let them know about our progress. I thank them both again, and they're just thrilled. Neither can believe that we made it that far and that the car held up.

Neither can we.

As we pulled into our driveway, I saw Joanna and I exhaled for what felt like the first time all day. Relief washed over me like a cold wave, and the tension melted off my body. The relief wasn't just in making it home—it was in knowing that we did it. That we conquered the road. That the battle was over.

Joanna knew the story and had been getting updates all day as well. And seeing her standing there, waving as if she, too, had been holding her breath, made pulling in feel a little more like crossing the finish line in a marathon. And yes, she was in disbelief that we made it as she saw, heard, and smelled the car.

"You made it all the way up here in this? Holy cow!"

When I went to bed that night, I thought about what had just happened. As I lay there, I replayed every shake of the wheel, every stranger who stepped up, and every risk we endured. It wasn't just about getting from point A to point B—it was about embracing uncertainty and finding grace in unexpected places. And I realized that sometimes trusting the road ahead, even when you can't see around the bend, is where real growth happens.

But one thing kept coming back to me—the guy who made this whole thing happen.

Because, really, I thought about what I would have done had this guy not stepped up. The challenges we would have faced. The moments we would have missed. And the people I would have let down. It was bigger than just offering a solution—it was that he modeled something worth modeling.

The truth is, many times in life, we end up on the short end of the stick. We feel like we have no options, and sometimes we don't. It takes sharing our situation with others in the community for there even to be a chance.

And that's when it happens.

What's the "it" you say? The "it" is when people come together to help their neighbors. When tough times get shared, when prayers get prayed, and people push forward despite the risks and challenges.

Did we make it home in time for her tournament? Absolutely. Was it meaningful to her? Without a doubt. Did she play well? For her first high-school tournament, she was terrific!

We came home that day with more than just a car that defied the odds—we arrived with a renewed faith in people and the power of community. This journey taught me that no matter how bumpy or uncertain the road gets, kindness and a willingness to push forward can make the most challenging journey feel like a victory worth celebrating.

Oh, and one last point. The guy who made this whole thing happen—his name is George. And the car he arranged for us—it was a Legacy.

And here's the tie-in.

George's gift wasn't just the Legacy—it was the LEGACY he leaves behind with every life he touches. True legacies aren't just the stories people tell about you, but the impact you leave on the lives you touch. George showed us that in a world that often feels too fast, furious, and indifferent, caring for others isn't just an action—it's a legacy worth living.

MAKING IT MATTER

Essence of the Moment

Sometimes the road ahead feels impossible, but the people who step in and care make the journey worth taking. George didn't just give us a car—he gave us a chance, reminding us that legacies are built through kindness and connection.

Timeless Truths

- ☑ **Hope Drives Forward:** Even the roughest roads can be navigated when fueled by faith and determination.
- ☑ **Kindness Transforms Lives:** Simple acts of generosity can create lasting ripples of impact.
- ☑ **Legacies Are Built Daily:** What you do for others today becomes the foundation of tomorrow's stories.

Bringing It Home

1. **Practice Everyday Generosity:** Find small ways to support someone in need—a kind word, a thoughtful gesture, or practical help can make all the difference.

2. **Celebrate the Helpers:** Take a moment to recognize and thank those who step up when things get tough, whether in your life or your community.
3. **Embrace Imperfection:** Remember that taking a leap of faith, even when the odds seem stacked against you, often leads to the most meaningful outcomes.

Next Level Thinking

Ask yourself:
▷ How has someone's kindness impacted your life in a way you'll never forget?
▷ What steps can you take to ensure your actions reflect the legacy you hope to leave?
▷ In times of uncertainty, how can you lean on faith and community to move forward?
▷ Who in your life needs to know how much their support has meant to you?

Insight to Remember

"True legacies aren't just the stories people tell about you, but the impact you leave on the lives you touch."

10

UNMASKING THE TRUTH

Honesty can be a gift... or a grenade. It all depends on how it's received.

A good friend reached out after reading what I wrote about *measuring worth*. Her initial message was simple: "What do you think of me?"

But her follow-up statement stopped me cold: "Be brutally honest. Good, bad, or indifferent. I really want to know."

Oh, no, not good. Not only did I hesitate, I tried to talk her out of it. Because honesty isn't always easy, and it certainly isn't kind.

She continued with her plea, "Just once, I'd like to hear what someone really thinks of me and not because they are my friend, family, boss, coworker, etc. I want to know what they really see."

This wasn't just random curiosity—it was a plea for clarity. The kind of plea that comes from someone who's searching for missing puzzle pieces.

And so, against my better judgment, I accepted.

An hour later, I bit my lip, buckled down, and started writing. Letters dripped onto the keyboard and seemingly self-assembled. Word after word, thought after thought, the document became flooded with bullets, quotes, and perceptions of her.

I asked again if she really wanted to know and if she could handle the honesty. She replied, "Good, bad or whatever, please share."

So, for two and a half hours, I threw everything I could think of at the keyboard: things I admired, what I noticed, what I thought could be better, and what I really thought about her. After I read the twelve lengthy paragraphs in their final form, I froze.

No way I could just send this to someone and let them sort through it all. I cringed and shook my head in disbelief. And I wasn't just cringing; I was truly nervous about how it would be received. So I chose not to send it.

Enter, Joanna.

When Joanna first heard what I had agreed to she had that kind of look that said, *good luck on that!* Then she laughed and walked away.

Now, I was forcing her to get involved. "I don't want to read that," she quips.

"Please. I need you to put yourself in her shoes and tell me what you'd do if you were her. And how you'd take this."

She then gave me one of those looks that said, *Okay, but if this backfires on you, I'm not fixing it.*

And so, against her better judgment, she accepted.

Five minutes of radio silence later and Joanna says, "Wow. This is SO good and real. She's gonna cry, but I don't think it will be a bad cry. Just emotion. It's a lot to take in if she connects with this."

"So I should send it?" I asked.

"You should send it. I can't imagine anyone ever giving her this kind of feedback—even a therapist."

Joanna's response gave me the courage I needed. I asked my friend again if she was sure she wanted it, and her response was a resounding "Yes."

I gave her one final warning: "Once you see this, you can't un-see it. It's honest and what I truly think and feel."

She acknowledged the warning and said, "I'm a big girl. I can handle it."

With a great deal of trepidation and one of the deepest breaths I'd ever taken, I almost hit send. My finger just sat there and hovered above the button for what seemed like an eternity.

Then, I closed my eyes, scrunched my face, opened them, and hit send.

It shouldn't have been that hard, but it was. And I could have done any number of things, but instead, I just sat there, waiting for a response. Every second seemed to drag on. Seconds turned into minutes, and before long, the five-minute mark hit, and it felt like it had been five hours. I kept looking at my phone and waiting for something. Anything.

Then, the dots appeared. She was typing her response. Then they stopped. Then they started again. My heart was pounding as I tuned everything else out and wondered if I'd taken it too far. Will it hurt her? Will she understand my perspective? Will this end our friendship?

My heart was legit about to jump out of my chest.

Ding!

Her reply was short but powerful—and Joanna was right. "You are so spot on that tears are now running down my face." She added, "Thank you for being honest. I think even more of you now."

Then, something else happened. She made a comment that stayed with me. She told me she was going to print out what I wrote and keep it in her bible, where she keeps all her treasures.

If I had to guess, I'd say that part hit me much harder than I thought it would. Knowing I helped shine a light where it was desperately needed and providing personal and meaningful feedback to someone who truly valued it was one of the most satisfying feelings I've ever had.

But there was something else, too.

That day wasn't just about feedback but about bravery, honesty, and courage. The kind of bravery that compels you to face the truth, no matter how uncomfortable it is, and use it to grow. My friend reminded me that honesty isn't always kind, but it's always worth it. And when we courageously ask for help and accept it, we take a small step closer to becoming the best version of ourselves.

Moments like this aren't just rare—they're transformative. They often show up as gifts in unassuming packages that we have to be willing to open and accept. And when we do, look out...

MAKING IT MATTER

Honesty can be a painful gift, but it holds the power to illuminate and transform. Bravery in asking for—and receiving—the truth is the first step toward growth and self-discovery.

Timeless Truths

- ☑ **Honesty Reveals Growth:** The truth, even when uncomfortable, is a catalyst for transformation.
- ☑ **Feedback Takes Courage:** Asking for and accepting raw, honest feedback requires vulnerability and strength.
- ☑ **Truth Builds Truth:** Honest conversations, when approached with care and empathy, strengthen relationships and deepen mutual respect.

Bringing It Home

1. **Be a Truth Teller:** If someone asks for your honest opinion, take the time to respond with both truth and kindness. Reflect on how your feedback can encourage growth while respecting their feelings.
2. **Ask for Feedback:** Choose one trusted person this week and ask for their insight into an area of your life where you'd like to improve. Approach the conversation with curiosity and openness, knowing it's a step closer to becoming your best self.
3. **Honor Vulnerability:** Look for an opportunity this month to acknowledge and celebrate someone's courage in seeking the truth. Let them know how much you admire their bravery and willingness to grow.

Next Level Thinking

Ask yourself:

▷ How do you typically respond to honest feedback, and how might you improve your openness to it?

▷ Who might benefit from your honest perspective, and how can you share it with care?

▷ What prevents you from seeking raw, honest feedback, and how can you overcome that barrier?

▷ In what ways can facing uncomfortable truths help you grow into your best self?

Insight to Remember

"Honesty isn't always kind, but it's always worth it. And when we courageously ask for help and accept it, we take a small step closer to becoming the best version of ourselves"

11

THE RIGHT AUDIENCE

What if finding the right audience could change everything?

By 2020, the world felt disconnected. In-person conversations became rare, and online interactions grew more divisive. Social media was flooded with arguments, echo chambers, and negativity.

But instead of stepping away, I turned to writing—not just to share updates or what I was eating, but to connect. To foster understanding. To help people see our similarities instead of our differences.

At first, it felt good. I wrote about experiences, emotions, and the lessons I was learning—and there were a lot. I wrote stories with context—little windows into my life and the world around me.

Friends and family engaged, but over time, something shifted. My posts stopped reaching people. The algorithms weren't kind to positivity or questions about narratives, and since I wasn't sparking mass controversy, my content fell into the void.

By 2022, it was as if I'd all but disappeared. My frustrations grew. Writings I'd worked hard on didn't even reach my closest family members.

Something had to give.

Then, a call from Ms. Bonnie—a lifelong friend and second mom to me. She'd been a part of my life for over thirty years and always had a knack for encouragement. She was one of the ones I'd write specifically for, and she always wanted to know more. Bonnie had also noticed the shift in my visibility, but instead of letting me stay frustrated, she offered a solution.

"I found an amazing group on Facebook," she said, her voice as enthusiastic as ever. "It's centered around positivity. You'll love the people there—they're kind, funny, and they love stories like yours."

She sent me an invite, and I accepted. But for a couple of months, I didn't get involved. I'd scroll through posts occasionally, liking a few here and there, but I didn't participate.

Honestly, I wasn't sure anyone would engage with a complete stranger.

Then, one night, after a somewhat disappointing lack of engagement from family and friends, I decided to join in. I used the same story from a couple of hours earlier just to test the waters.

It was about Joanna and me fixing a washing machine. A simple story, really—full of the typical antics and mishaps that come with home repairs. One I'd written the way I always do—with humor, honesty, and a little heart.

And that was the moment it happened.

My first post in this group of strangers ended up with over two hundred reactions and more than a hundred comments. It wasn't "viral" by internet standards, but for me, it was extraordinary.

These weren't just likes—they were invitations to connect. Strangers were engaging with my writings in a way I'd never experienced before.

They asked questions, shared their own stories, and encouraged me to write more.

For the first time in years, I felt seen. Validated. Inspired.

Over the next two weeks, I'd end up posting eight stories. Each was met with even more enthusiasm than the last. Thousands of reactions. Hundreds of comments.

I spent countless hours responding to people, answering questions, and diving into conversations—about everything!

It was both exhausting and exhilarating at the same time!

"Why are you spending so much time writing to strangers?" Joanna asked one evening, her tone a mix of curiosity and mild annoyance.

"Because I found a group of people starving for connection—just like me," I said.

The group had one simple rule: posts had to be positive. That rule forced me to dig deeper. To focus only on the good. It was refreshing and much needed with all the negativity going on.

So, for the next several weeks, I sifted through hundreds of my stories, cherry-picking the best ones to share with the group. That process gave birth to something unexpected: the makings of a book.

That's how my book *Cherry Picking the Good* got its name. It was born out of a group of strangers who believed in me at a time when I barely believed in myself.

What I didn't realize before joining that group was how important the right audience is for whatever message you want to share. My family and friends cared, but as a whole, they weren't the right audience for my stories, although some were.

It wasn't until I stepped outside my comfort zone that I saw the type of impact my writings could have.

Sometimes, it takes a stranger to see us for who we really are. A kind word from someone who recognizes your potential can change everything.

For me, it was a group of strangers on Facebook who opened the door to possibility and gave me the courage to walk through it. There was Wendy, Maureen, Stacy, and Kathy. Kalin, and Judy, Kim, Rita, and Maggie. Lauri, Melissa, Joan, Linda, Stephanie, and Mary. And Marlene, Renee, Sandy, Marilyn, Aleta, Gma JoAn, Tammy, Cindy, and Teresa. Lisa, Leah, Janice, Cathy, Patricia, Diane, Denise, Elaine, Becky, and Joanna. And I can't forget Lois, Lori, Laura, Niki, Penny, Ruth, Susan, Susi, Jane, Jody, Harriet, Toni, Yvette, Molly, Dennise, Debbie, Debra, and Deborah—just to name a few.

The way they welcomed me matters, too. They treated me with kindness and encouragement from the very first post, and that made all the difference.

It's a lesson I carry with me now: how we treat others—especially when they're new—can absolutely shape their path forward. In other words, the right audience can, in fact, change everything.

If I hadn't taken that leap and shared my story with strangers, I might have stopped writing altogether. But because of their encouragement, I kept going. And in the process, I learned something profound: connection isn't about the size of your audience— it's about finding the people who truly value what you have to say.

So here's to the strangers who remind us of our worth and become friends. To the ones who show up when we need them most. And to the power of connection, even in the unlikeliest of places.

MAKING IT MATTER

Essence of the Moment

Sometimes, the people closest to us aren't the ones who can see us most clearly. Finding the right audience isn't just about being heard —it's about discovering the courage to keep sharing your voice.

Timeless Truths

☑ **The Right Audience Matters:** Sure, your message matters, but finding those who truly value it is what brings it to life.

☑ **Connection Fuels Creativity:** Encouragement from the right people can reignite passion and purpose.

☑ **Strangers Can Uplift:** Unexpected kindness from new faces can profoundly shape your journey.

Bringing It Home

1. **Step Outside Comfort:** Take an hour today to research online communities or local groups that align with your interests. Joining just one could lead you to an audience that truly connects with your passions.

2. **Be the Encourager:** The next time you see someone share their creative work, leave a thoughtful comment or message them. This week, aim to inspire at least one person to keep going with their craft.
3. **Celebrate the Small Wins:** Reflect on your achievements over the next month, no matter how minor they seem. Write down one or two moments of connection that made an impact, and let them fuel your motivation moving forward.

Next Level Thinking

Ask yourself:
- Have you found an audience that truly values your voice? If not, where might you look?
- How do you respond to feedback—especially when it comes from someone outside your inner circle?
- How can you use your experiences to uplift and encourage others?
- What risks are you willing to take to find the connections that inspire you to grow?

Insight to Remember

"Connection isn't about the size of your audience—it's about finding the people who truly value what you have to say."

12

SHELTER IN THE STORM

Within seconds of walking in, I noticed a beautiful golden retriever.

He was drinking from a makeshift water bowl from one of the displays that looked like it had just been repurposed.

Not what I expected from a consignment store, yet it's strangely calming. The lady behind the desk welcomes me, then immediately goes and tends to "Duke." The way she comforts him catches my attention.

She repeatedly tells him how beautiful he is and how it will all be okay. Kind of strange to hear, so I tuned in even more.

It continues, and so does her attentiveness to him.

A good ten minutes goes by, and I'm browsing along and looking through women's clothing. I have four ladies in my house who always enjoy the randomness I find when I'm out, and that's when the phone call came in.

"This is Michelle—how can I help you?" I hear. Then, "Oh, great. I'm so glad you got my message, Jeff. I have Duke here with me at my store, and I'm REALLY enjoying him."

She gives the guy directions, tells him she'll see him shortly, and ends the call. And that's when I chimed in.

"I take it Duke isn't your dog?"

"Oh my gosh, I wish. He's so gorgeous. Just look at him! I found him out in the middle of the road during that terrible storm this morning—I just had to stop and pick him up."

Duke had a collar and a phone number, so she made the call and took him to work with her. That was a couple of hours ago.

For the next half-hour, I witnessed an incredible display of love and affection towards animals. The kind you only see from someone who's been broken or seen animals harmed, and they have a special place in their hearts for them.

Michelle tells me about her background with horses and the kind of family she grew up with, and it starts clicking. She loves taking care of animals and wants them to have the best life they can while they're here. It was truly inspiring to see and hear.

The bells on the door start clashing, and in walks some guy, in a hurry. So much so that he left his Jeep door open and lights on. And it's still raining.

"And you must be Jeff?" Michelle calls out.

"Yep. Where's Duke?" he says in a very bothered tone.

Michelle quickly squats down, kisses Duke on the head while rubbing him, and says, "Time to go." Then she walks him out from behind the desk and hands Jeff the leash.

Before I get to this next part, I'd like to point out that how people treat animals matters. You can learn a lot about someone just by watching how they interact. Dogs, cats, horses, birds, doesn't matter. It's all important and can provide a multitude of clues that help reveal their character as well as what they've seen and lived.

Okay, back to the story.

"Let's go!" I hear, as Jeff yanks the leash and storms off towards the door. Then, "I don't have time for this, Duke," as he scurries out the door, nearly dragging Duke behind.

Seconds later, he's loaded up and gone, and Michelle breaks into tears. She was SO upset and wished she had never called him. And she couldn't believe the way he treated Duke and how Duke just cowered when he saw Jeff.

"Oh my gosh, I'm just sick to my stomach," she tells me.

It was her reactions, emotions, and compassion that sold me, not her clothes. By that, I mean we're in a consignment store, so you just have to keep up.

You see, consignment stores are a dime a dozen. I've been to many, and they all have the same kind of layout. The same kind of lifeless feel. The same kind of markups and sales and whatnot. But they don't have Michelle.

I had about three hours to kill that day, and all three of them died right there in her store. While shopping, I watched Michelle dance her dance with customer after customer, and she made people feel like they mattered. Michelle has an eye for style and a love for clothing that combines well with her straight-to-the-point mannerisms that make people feel great, time after time.

Before I left, I told her, "You're the kind of person my wife would just love. For so many reasons." She laughed but could see that I was serious.

I showed up again the next week, but this time, it was with my wife in tow. "Joanna, this is Michelle. The one I told you about. Michelle, this is my wife, Joanna. The one I told you about."

And that, friends, is where this story ended, and a new story began. One they're both in without me: a tale of friendship with all sorts of highlights, meet-ups, adventures, tears, hugs, animals, and wine.

In a way, their story is beautiful, just like Duke. And they've found their own "Shelter in the Storm" in each other, just the way Duke found it that day.

MAKING IT MATTER

Compassion has the power to transform even the simplest spaces into sanctuaries. In life's storms, the shelter we find in others can leave a lasting mark and create unexpected new beginnings.

Timeless Truths

- ☑ **Kindness Reveals Character:** How we treat others—especially animals—speaks volumes about who we are.
- ☑ **Compassion Inspires Connection:** Small acts of care can create ripples that bring people together in profound ways.
- ☑ **Friendship is Shelter:** The bonds we form can provide a haven during life's tempests.

Bringing It Home

1. **Practice Compassion Daily:** Take a moment today to notice someone or something that could benefit from your care. It might be offering help to a neighbor, feeding a stray animal, or simply giving someone your full attention.
2. **Celebrate the Helpers:** Think of someone who regularly shows compassion, like Michelle did for Duke. This week, reach out to thank them or recognize their kindness in a way that makes them feel valued.
3. **Create a Safe Space:** Make a conscious effort this month to be a source of support for someone going through a tough time. Whether it's listening without judgment or offering a helping hand, your empathy can make a lasting impact.

Next Level Thinking

Ask yourself:

▷ How do you respond to situations where kindness and compassion are needed?

▷ Who in your life embodies the kind of care and connection Michelle showed?

▷ What can you do to make someone or something feel safe and valued today?

▷ How might building new connections lead to transformative friendships in your own life?

Insight to Remember

"How people treat animals matters. You can learn a lot about someone just by watching how they interact. Dogs, cats, horses, birds, doesn't matter."

13

A MOMENT OF WEAKNESS

Life-changing moments can happen in an instant—and sometimes, that instant stretches across days—or months. This one began in our living room, moved to the bedroom, and ramped up once Maria showed up a few hours later.

"My arms are really heavy for some reason," I said to Joanna, grimacing as we practiced what we were planning to teach the next morning.

I'd spent the week working with Tonya and had been in and out of Congressional briefings. Round-the-clock workdays happened occasionally and there had been a few this week. There was also a surgery the day before for my second-born and all the stressors that came with it as I was right there by her side.

Exhaustion was par for the course I was playing, but this felt different.

By 8pm, I was lying in bed, struggling to open and close my hands. Everything hurt. My legs felt leaden, my breath grew shallow, and a clamp seemed to have settled onto my chest. As the hours dragged on, my mind began to race, trying to make sense of it. But my body wasn't willing to cooperate.

Joanna, always the quick thinker, called our neighbor, Maria. Within minutes, Maria was at our front door to help me get into her car, as we were emergency room bound.

I'd hoped for answers, but instead, I found myself in the hospital under the glow of harsh fluorescent lights, bombarded by a parade of doctors and nurses. The poking, prodding, and scanning went on through the night. I was beyond exhausted, teetering on the edge of delirium, but there was no rest to be found.

The next day, it got worse. Nothing worked. My strength evaporated. Holding a pen became impossible. My muscles felt as though they were disintegrating from the inside out.

"This doesn't make sense," one of the doctors muttered, shaking his head as he stared at my charts. "What we're seeing is something we only encounter in patients with severely compromised immune systems."

Joanna then took the time to share what my previous five years had entailed—including the one hundred and twenty-hour workweeks that were my norm. They were stunned.

The diagnosis? A muscle-eating virus that had turned my body into its battleground. They told me my muscle enzyme levels were through the roof—levels that should have been fatal. Yet there I was, still hanging in there.

Later that day, I was drained—physically, mentally, and emotionally. The pain was relentless, and the doctors were cautious with their optimism—to the extent that there wasn't much at all. Then came the moment that changed everything.

Lying in my hospital bed, I overheard my eldest say something that pierced through the fog of exhaustion, "Does this mean I'll never get to play with Daddy again?" This, while looking up at Joanna and clinging to her leg.

It wasn't just a question—it was a challenge to me. A reminder of what was at stake. I closed my eyes and replayed her voice over and over for days. It became my anchor and my motivation to fight harder than I ever had.

When I was finally discharged, things were different. I wasn't the same person who had walked into the ER—not in the least. My body was frail, my muscles were depleted, and my thoughts were scattered.

More so, I struggled to walk, talk, and eat without complications. The doctors explained how the virus had wiped out whatever was left of my immune system, leaving me the equivalent of what a newborn would have.

At first, I chalked up my post-hospital struggles to recovery. But eating became an ordeal, quickly—one that was new to me.

My nose ran, my eyes teared up, and my throat tightened with every bite. Testing revealed a grim reality: I had developed severe allergies to nearly thirty different things, seven of which were life-threatening. Grass, of all things, was one of the seven and so was cottonseed oil—a staple in restaurant cooking.

Not good. Mowing my lawn was no longer an option, nor was dining out. If I was to survive without an EpiPen, everything I ate had to be prepared at home. Joanna, who had never been much of a cook, stepped up and into the kitchen in the most remarkable way.

She dove into recipe books, experimented with ingredients, and learned from every source she could get ahold of. Our kitchen had been transformed into a sanctuary of clean eating. Within weeks, she was a chef in her own right, crafting meals that nourished and healed all of us—and, namely, me.

But food wasn't the only challenge. Sleep became a battle I couldn't win. Desperate, I turned to medication. Ambien seemed like a miracle at first—until I accidentally discovered its dark side.

One morning I bumped into some friends of mine at Starbucks. The guy casually mentioned how funny I'd been the other night. "What do you mean?" I asked, confused. I hadn't seen them in months. But they had photos—photos of me. At their house. Two nights earlier.

Sleepwalking, it turned out, was a side-effect of the medication. I was horrified, especially since that was the first of many instances I found out about where I had no memory whatsoever.

I stopped taking the medication immediately, opting instead for sheer physical exhaustion to force myself to sleep. That's where Chad came in—a highly recommended trainer at my local gym with a background in kinesiology. He helped me rebuild my strength, one step at a time, and showed me how to move forward—both physically and mentally.

Six months after my trip to the hospital, my life looked entirely different. Joanna had mastered the art of cooking, and our family had embraced clean eating. Exercise became a cornerstone of our daily routine, and our kids were also reaping the benefits.

I'd also learned to navigate life with allergies and developed a deep empathy for others who lived with similar challenges. And I had a newfound respect for the power of medicines and vowed never to compromise my mind like that again.

But the most significant change? My priority. I cut my work hours to less than a fourth of what they were, and dedicated myself to being present with my family. I saw opportunities for connection I'd once overlooked, and I grabbed them with both hands.

You see, life has a way of surprising us—sometimes in the hardest ways imaginable. If we look deep enough into those moments of struggle, we find seeds of transformation. For me, this was a chance to reset, rebuild, and realign my life with my values—again.

That moment didn't just change me—it saved me. It gave me hope and the will to create the kind of life for my family they'll always remember—one I'm a part of.

And, to bring this one full circle, there's something else.

Moments of weakness often feel like endings, but they can also be beginnings. This one reminded me that even in our most vulnerable states, we hold the power to create something new—something better—not just for ourselves, but for those that matter most.

MAKING IT MATTER

Moments of weakness can take us to the edge, but they can also challenge us to rebuild stronger and more aligned with what matters most. In vulnerability, we discover the power to create a life of meaning and connection.

Timeless Truths

- ☑ **Weakness Reveals Strength:** True resilience is forged in the moments when we feel our weakest.
- ☑ **Crisis Spurs Change:** Life's most complex challenges often lead us to reevaluate and realign our priorities.
- ☑ **Healing is a Journey:** Rebuilding takes time, intention, and the support of those who stand by us.

Bringing It Home

1. **Identify a Priority Today:** Write down one area of your life that feels out of alignment with your values. Take one small step today to bring it back into balance, like scheduling dedicated family time or revisiting a goal.
2. **Embrace a Healthier Choice:** Choose one meal this week to prepare at home with clean, nourishing ingredients. Make it a family activity to connect while prioritizing your health.
3. **Reach Out for Connection:** This month, schedule a conversation with someone who supports you—a mentor, family member, or friend—and share a goal or struggle you're working through. Their perspective could be invaluable to you going forward.

Next Level Thinking

Ask yourself:

- How can moments of struggle help reveal what truly matters in your life?
- What areas of your life might need realignment to better reflect your values?
- Who are the people you lean on during hard times, and how can you show your gratitude for their support?
- How might embracing vulnerability allow you to connect more deeply with others?

Insight to Remember

"Even in our most vulnerable states, we hold the power to create something new—something better—not just for ourselves, but for those that matter most."

14

THE CIRCLE OF FRIENDS

The bond of friendship that shall not be broken.
The centerpiece on our living room table—right there in the middle of everything is a piece of art. Not just any piece of art, but one that cleverly shows the interlocking of hands from people in a circle.

When we had our "going away party" in 2016, it was a gift that was delivered with tears. First from her, then from us. It wasn't just heartwarming—it was heart-wrenching.

This, from a lady our kids had affectionately named Ms. Jan.

She'd watched our little ones grow up and participated in their lives. She'd go on walks with us, host pool parties, play in the street with them—and they all just adored her.

But it didn't start out that way.

The Hatfields and McCoys had a history of feuds—and so did my grandparents and Tom. They were next-door neighbors, but they were anything but neighborly. When my grandmother passed, Joanna and I bought the house from the estate and inherited a neighbor known for being intolerant.

At least that's what I had always been told—both from my grandmother and my parents, who had seen and lived through whatever problem there was.

When we moved in, I attempted to be friendly with Tom, but he wanted nothing to do with us. That version of him could best be described as the Grinch with a grudge. Sadly, whatever grudge he had against my grandparents and parents had extended to us.

Soon after we moved in, Jan entered the scene and started frequenting his house. Jan was friendly, warm, and loving—the opposite of our perception of Tom. Jan would wave at passers-by and do her best to connect with everyone within earshot of her.

I'll never forget the day Jan brought a basket of cookies over just before Thanksgiving. Joanna was in the middle of making salsa, and her blender had just died with all the tomatoes still inside. Not three minutes later, Jan was back with her VitaMix and helping transfer everything over.

"Prepare to be mind-blown," Jan said with the excitement of a child. "This thing is going to knock your socks off!"

Joanna didn't ask for help, but when Jan heard opportunity knocking, she didn't just let it in—she laid out the red carpet for it. Not just that, she also brought a bottle of wine with her, and when it opened, it didn't stop pouring. Of course, I'm talking about her heart —because that's what we saw open that day.

Jan knew the history, but she regularly told us how she was working on Tom. She wanted him to see us for who we were and not as those he had problems with. It was a process, but she was determined. Week after week, she kept planting little seeds.

Small changes began to surface. Tom lingered a little longer during conversations. He'd wave hello when we'd come home in the afternoons. He'd say, "Good morning, Shawn!" when I saw him getting the paper.

Within months, that grudge Tom was holding onto had all but disappeared. Little by little, Tom would let his guard down and say something helpful. A genuine smile replaced his scowl, and I could see that it tickled him whenever he knew something I didn't.

And yet, he shared his knowledge with me and offered advice only a seasoned pro could give. First, about mowers, then about grass—"You know, if you cut it a little higher, it'll handle the summer heat better."

Not just advice, but wisdom. He shared his experiences and the mistakes he'd made in the hopes of it connecting—and it did.

He especially enjoyed talking "cars" with my son due to how

quickly Paxton grasped concepts and wanted to try to fix them on his own. Each time, we'd see Jan just sitting back and enjoying what she'd helped create.

Holidays became special because Jan had a unique way of making our kids feel seen, loved, and cared for in a way that was usually only seen in direct families.

Oh, and it wasn't just on holidays, it was every day. She was supportive of all the little things—good grades in school, jump-roping in the street, new outfits that seemed odd: didn't matter—she loved it all and showed up for the kids even when she had her own pain and struggles.

Past that, Jan always had thoughtful questions and would sit and listen for hours. It wasn't always listening, either; that lady could talk—she was SO interesting and had the craziest stories. One night, she needed an ear, and I gave it. We sat out on our driveway and had drinks. The more she talked, the more I drank. The more I drank, the less I "drank" as it was mostly Coke Zero—and I paid the price.

The price was three days in bed—for me. Not because of the "drinks," but because of the aspartame. Who knew aspartame poisoning was a thing? Not me, until then. That was the last time I ever drank soda—and I thank her for it.

Stories of her childhood and "wild child" days were eye-opening and breathtaking. That whole Woodstock era—yeah, that was her in a nutshell. Peace, love, and unity—for all. She carried those lessons with her and actively taught others kindness and caring just by living the life she lived.

As the years passed, our bond grew: mine, hers, Joanna's, and Tom's. We'd visit more and more and help each other in ways some say are just being good neighbors, but it was beyond that. We cared about them, and them about us. Sickness became everyone's problem. Death of a loved one was felt by all. A problem with something—anything—became a conversation.

So when we told them we were moving, they were crushed. Saddened probably fits the bill better. They helped us prepare in every possible way, and Jan even helped lead the effort the day we sold our house.

Day after day, she'd check on us, bring us wine, and help pack boxes and load them up. She didn't want us to leave, nor did we want to leave her, but life sometimes leads us in directions we don't understand.

Then, our going away party happened, and that's when she brought the box. Jan was standing there with Tom, and she wanted us all to see what was in it at the same time. "This isn't just for your new house," she said. "It's for you to remember all of the memories we've shared... together."

Joanna opened the box carefully and took out the most beautiful sculpture, and the gasps started. We heard "Awe," "I love it," and "It's beautiful" from the kids, but then Joanna picked up on something even more significant and shared it with everyone.

"Look how perfect this is!" she said, holding it up so everyone could see while pointing something else out. "There are eight people holding hands in a perfect circle—one for each of us and one each for Ms. Jan and Mr. Tom."

And that's when Jan's tears started a cascading effect.

What Jan had done was create a circle of friendship that went beyond being neighbors. She showed us all the power of love and the beauty in connection. People mattered to Jan, and her ability to show it was inspiring.

We also saw Tom's heart grow three sizes that day. When Joanna pointed out the eight people, Tom's face changed. His jaw tightened, his eyes glossed over, and for the first and only time, we saw tears spill onto his cheeks. In that moment, I saw not just a neighbor, but a man who had finally let go of years of bitterness and opened his heart fully.

It was a moment of healing—for him and for us.

That sculpture is now a reminder of what Jan taught us: that love is patient, kindness is contagious, and grudges are too heavy to carry. Tom may have started as the Grinch next door, but Jan's quiet, persistent love transformed him—and all of us.

It's proof that family isn't just who you're born into; it's who you choose—and who chooses you back.

That bond of friendship—the circle of hands—will forever remind us that connection and love are at the heart of what truly matters.

And yes, it's still the centerpiece in our living room today.

MAKING IT MATTER

Essence of the Moment

Friendship is a bond that transcends differences, heals wounds, and creates lasting memories. Through love and connection, even the most closed-off hearts can open to something beautiful.

Timeless Truths

- ☑ **Love Builds Bridges:** Compassion and persistence can overcome even the deepest divides.
- ☑ **Kindness is Transformative:** Acts of care, no matter how small, can change lives in unexpected ways.
- ☑ **Friendship is Chosen Family:** True friends are the ones who show up, no matter the circumstance.

Bringing It Home

1. **Reach Out Today:** Call or visit a neighbor, friend, or loved one you haven't connected with in a while. Share a story or a simple "thinking of you" to brighten their day.

2. **Show Unexpected Kindness:** This week, do something thoughtful for someone, like baking cookies, lending a hand, or offering to listen—small gestures can make a significant impact.
3. **Create a Reminder of Connection:** This month, craft or purchase something meaningful to symbolize the relationships that matter most to you—like a photo frame, keepsake, or note of gratitude.

Next Level Thinking

Ask yourself:

▷ Who in your life has been a "Ms. Jan," quietly but persistently showing care and connection?
▷ What small act of kindness can you do today to make someone feel seen and valued?
▷ How might you mend a strained relationship by choosing compassion and patience?
▷ What reminders do you have in your life of the connections that shape who you are?

Insight to Remember

"Love is patient, kindness is contagious, and grudges are too heavy to carry."

15

REALIZING POTENTIAL

The chair sat empty.

By now, I should have been welcoming our newest hire. Instead, it was nine o'clock on a Monday morning, and he was nowhere to be found.

"Have you heard anything from the new guy?" I inquired.

"Not a thing!" Joanna replied.

The day before, he'd impressed me with his knack for design, inspiring sample work, and ideas for growing the business. But beneath the surface, there was a noticeable hesitation—almost as if he wasn't sure of himself.

As for the time, I'm certain we had agreed on eight-thirty as his starting hours. I know because I double-checked what I wrote down while sitting with him, and he confirmed.

I've seen my share of oddities on the first day, like when that one guy showed up high as a kite. Or the lady who immediately started organizing other people's desks while they were gone. Yep, bizarre.

But not showing up? That was a new one. It's now nine-thirty, and there's no answer on his phone, nor is there any communication whatsoever. And this is a guy we were hiring to do a mixture of customer service, web design, and graphics for us. It just didn't make sense. Was he okay?

Prior to hiring this guy, we'd probably spoken some ten times. So, when there was an empty chair where I thought he'd be sitting, something felt off.

Ten o'clock rolls around, and nothing. Eleven, and now I'm really bothered and questioning all of our previous communications. I called again—no answer. I sent a text message—no reply. I sent an email—crickets.

The clock struck noon, and within seconds, the phone rang.

"I'm sorry, Mr. Shawn, I got all your messages, and I wanted to at least give you the courtesy of letting you know I'd changed my mind."

Turns out, he quit—before he ever started.

"I just don't think it's going to work out," he said, with his voice trembling.

I was stunned, and I had a hard time swallowing. My heart sank, and I fought back the urge to reply with emotion. So I was just silent.

"Mr. Shawn. Did you hear me?"

"I hear you," I said, my voice steady but my heart racing. "But I think you're making a mistake. People like you don't come along often, and I'm not ready to let you give up on yourself before you've even started."

Now *he* was stunned and didn't know what to say.

There was a brief pause where neither of us spoke. I spent that time searching for the right words, and then I found them: "You need someone who sees and values what you're capable of. And that someone is me."

That one did it. It pulled him back off the proverbial ledge. Not a minute later, he hung up after saying he'd be there the next day. At eight-thirty.

When he walked in the following day, his nervous smile was noticeable. But behind it was a firm handshake, a laugh that was more likable than most, and an attitude that said, *I'm ready for something to go right*.

That was the moment I met Clayton. The real Clayton. Not the one he was pretending to be nor the one that was unsure of himself. Before that day, he was just a kid trying to find his way, and that's exactly what he found the day he started.

A year later, Clayton pulled me aside and said, "Thanks for making me come back." I knew he meant it.

Clayton turned out to be the epitome of what a hard-working, dedicated professional should be. He quickly became my go-to person due to his integrity and understanding of what it takes to turn ideas into reality.

Over the next five years, Clayton was consistently a top performer and one of our company's most valuable assets. Our talks turned to the kinds of companies he'd like to one day run. And so we worked through all sorts of concepts and tied as much of his skill-building to things he'd later use.

As our company started transitioning from development to maintenance, Clayton started building. He'd regularly run things past me and we worked together until his wings were ready to take flight.

Now, Clayton runs his own specialization company called IdeaSwell, and he's one of my most recommended people of all time to do business with. He's bright, articulate, and good on his word—an essential characteristic for anyone to have.

Looking back, I realize that moment wasn't just about convincing Clayton to show up—it was about helping him step into who he was meant to be. And when he told me, "Thanks for making me come back," I knew it wasn't just about a job. It was about building a foundation for the person he wanted to become.

Sometimes, the greatest impact we can have is simply refusing to let someone give up on themselves. What Clayton doesn't know is that he did the same for me. He reminded me of the power of persistence and how believing in someone—even when they can't see it themselves—can transform lives.

MAKING IT MATTER

Believing in someone when they're on the verge of giving up can spark profound transformation. Sometimes, all it takes is a little faith to help others—and ourselves—realize potential we didn't even know was there.

Timeless Truths

- ☑ **Faith Fuels Growth:** Believing in someone's potential can be the nudge they need to discover their capabilities.
- ☑ **Encouragement Changes Lives:** A kind word at the right moment can alter the trajectory of someone's journey.
- ☑ **Second Chances Change Everything:** Sometimes, offering someone the opportunity to try again can lead to growth, transformation, and unexpected success, revealing the power of persistence and belief in potential.

Bringing It Home

1. **Help Someone Believe:** Think about one person you could encourage today. Send a quick message, make a call, or have a conversation to remind them of their strengths.
2. **Invest in Future Growth:** Find a way to nurture someone's potential this week. Maybe you can teach them something new, give them honest feedback, or offer an opportunity to showcase their skills.
3. **Recognize the Ripple Effect:** By the end of the month, take time to reflect on how encouragement has shaped your own life. Write down or share a story about someone who believed in you and thank them if you haven't already.

Next Level Thinking

Ask yourself:

- ▷ Who in my life might benefit from someone believing in them right now, and how can I provide that support?
- ▷ How has encouragement at a pivotal moment shaped my own journey?
- ▷ How can I recognize and nurture the potential in someone who may not see it in themselves?
- ▷ What steps can I take to ensure I offer the same patience and encouragement I would hope to receive in moments of doubt?

Insight to Remember

"Sometimes, the greatest impact we can have is simply refusing to let someone give up on themselves."

16

A SUNRISE TO REMEMBER

Just as the sun started becoming visible, the sky illuminated the perfect color blend. A mad scramble ensued as we snapped pictures as quickly as we could—the sky, waves, birds, reeds, and shells—before the magic disappeared.

It was one of those rare moments that felt like it could last forever but seemingly vanished in the blink of an eye. A moment that will always hold a special place in my heart.

We were only five days into a two-thousand-mile trip, just me and my four kids, carving out two incredible weeks together in late 2020—our first stop: Myrtle Beach, SC.

"There's so much to do, and so little time!" McKenzie said, unknowingly summing up the trip—and life itself—perfectly.

After months of pandemic-induced isolation, we were exhausted. Masks, social distancing, and endless uncertainty had taken their toll, and this getaway wasn't just a break—it was a lifeline. For me and for them.

The first few days were a whirlwind of golf, frisbee on the beach, and long walks along the strip. We talked about life, practiced conversation skills, and learned lessons—each of us, in our own way.

From there, we headed south to the Tampa Bay area, retracing old steps and reliving memories.

"I can't believe you used to ride a unicycle this far!" my son said as we drove through my childhood neighborhood. I pointed out houses where my friends had lived and shared stories about the streets I used to roam.

"This house coming up on the left—yep, that one—that's where I broke my wrist jumping off a skateboard ramp."

We stopped by their old elementary school, snapping pictures and soaking in memories. "Remember when you came and taught my gifted class for a week, Dad?" Breanna said. "And there's where we had all those field day events—oh my gosh!"

Next up was the driving range, where they all learned golf. We found Coach Paul and spent the afternoon talking about how times have changed while showing off our new skills. A short drive later, we found our lifelong friends Mark and Micki, who welcomed us with open arms and endless hospitality.

Grandparents on both sides were next, and our dinners were filled with laughter, stories, and warmth you can only find around family. Our days, however, were ours. Driving, talking, walking on the beach—we found joy in the simple act of just being together.

Each stop along the way brought more connections, more laughter, and more tears. Back in our old neighborhood, we hugged old friends—Jan, Tom, John, Maria, Julia, and Chloe—and reminisced as though no time had passed.

"I'm exhausted, Dad, but I'm having a blast!" McKenzie exclaimed one evening, her grin giving her away. "It was so good to see Julia again."

The nights were just as full. We met with George, Dan, and Ms. Bonnie. Then we hung with Steph, Mia, and Betsy before bowling with Ms. May, who had gifts for each of the kids, as always. We shared ice cream at midnight and squeezed in as many moments with loved ones as time would allow.

This trip wasn't just about taking a break, it was about rediscovering the joy of our family and reconnecting with the people who'd shaped us.

In Orlando, Shawn and Breena made a surprise visit, driving hours with their family just to see us. Nicki invited us to Universal Studios the next day, where laughter echoed in every ride and every conversation. That evening, we met with my old college roommate, Chris, and his family, as well as our dear friend, Janene, and hers.

On the fifteen-hour drive home, the car was filled with singing, storytelling, and deep conversations about growing up, staying grounded, and finding joy in the journey.

Looking back through the photos, we were struck by the sheer volume of memories we'd assimilated. From the winding tunnels and rolling mountains to the beaches and coastlines, every image had a story of its own.

And then there were the sunrise and sunset pictures. At the time, the sun rising over the water in Myrtle Beach didn't seem like a big deal, just another beautiful moment in a trip full of them.

But now, that sunrise is more than a photo—it's a reminder.

It was the last trip we'd take together as the five of us before life moved forward and the kids started carving out their own paths. It's a picture that ended up on the cover of this book, symbolizing not just a trip but a pivotal moment in my life—and theirs.

That trip wasn't just a getaway—it was a gift that was opened a mile at a time. It was two thousand small moments wrapped into one life-changing experience.

You never know when a moment will come along that changes you forever. But you have to show up in the hope that it does.

This trip was one of those moments for me. It's a memory I'll carry with me—one that reminds me of the importance of time, connection, and simply being present.

It was, without question, the trip of a lifetime.

MAKING IT MATTER

Essence of the Moment

This trip wasn't just about a sunrise—it was about thousands of little moments strung together, creating something much bigger than any of us could have expected. It was a reminder that life's greatest gifts often come when we slow down and truly experience the journey.

Timeless Truths

- ☑ **Life Happens in the Small Moments:** The seemingly ordinary moments, when appreciated fully, often turn out to be the most extraordinary.
- ☑ **Shared Experiences Strengthen Bonds:** It's not about where you go or what you do—it's about who you're with and the memories you create together.
- ☑ **The Journey Matters:** Every mile, every stop, every conversation along the way shapes the bigger story of our lives.

Bringing It Home

1. **Savor a Moment:** Pause during your day to fully experience something simple—a cup of coffee, a conversation, or even a quiet moment outside. Let it sink in without distraction.
2. **Reconnect with Someone:** Reach out to a family member or friend and plan a time to share an experience this week—a walk, a meal, or even just a phone call. Focus on making that time meaningful.
3. **Plan a Journey to Remember:** Before the month ends, plan a trip or meaningful experience with your loved ones, big or small. It's about creating opportunities for connection, not the scale of the event.

Ask yourself:
- What small, seemingly ordinary moments in my life have left a lasting impact on me, and why?
- How can I create opportunities for deeper connections with the people I care about?
- What steps can I take to make sure I'm fully present during the journey, not just focused on the destination?
- How can I build a legacy of memories and connection that my loved ones will carry with them?

Insight to Remember

"You never know when a moment will come along that changes you forever. But you have to show up in the hope that it does."

17

THE PRETTIEST THING

What's prettier than happy?

Nothing. At least, according to my friend Abigail. And, having just seen her in a state of complete bliss, I have to agree.

The significance here is that Abigail is one of my favorite people. Her husband, David, just so happens to be another of my favorites. They're wildly different, but they're an excellent match. Oh, and they share the last name of Milby.

Fifteen minutes before I saw Abigail's bliss, I was standing at the customer service counter in the front of a Walmart. While standing in line and waiting, I struck up a conversation with one of the managers there named Adam. I asked if he had a minute to read something, and he said, "Sure."

I handed him my book and watched as he read a story in front of me. He was focused, but then I saw it connect. And his smile grew bigger and bigger... until he finished, looked up at me while nodding, and said, "Oh yeah, that's them!"

The story he read was Chapter 20—"Walmart People."

Thirty seconds later, we see David walking by, and he lights right up in a way that's unique to David. His eyes tell a story of joy and excitement, and his cheeks rise as though he's smiling big, but you just can't see it through his beard. He excitedly says, "Hey!! Look who it is!" and immediately comes over, reaches out to shake my hand, and greets Joanna.

Then, Abigail walks by as she is on her way to lunch, and when she looks up and notices all of us, she breaks into pure excitement. It really is her own special blend of happiness and energy that she brings with her everywhere. This impromptu meet-up was no different. She's so fun and welcoming. A better description is that she's remarkably engaging.

She told me how she received her copy of the book last week and read almost all of it. And that she read several chapters aloud to David. She said she couldn't believe how easy it was to read and how hard it was to put down.

And Abigail said she was going to order a second copy so she could give one to her mom... so her mom could see that her little girl was *good enough* to be featured in a book. How cool is that? And when I say she was excited, she was beaming!

Excitement was in the air, and all of her co-workers could see it. She even had David excited and hugged him right there on the spot. And then hugged us again.

I then asked if I could get a picture of the two of them and the book, and they agreed. "Click." Done.

She looks at the picture and says, "Oooh, I like that one... Nothing is prettier than happy!"

What an incredible, impromptu meet-up that was. We brought the book hoping we'd find them there, but it turned out way better than we imagined. Seeing what it meant to them for someone to recognize their "good" qualities was a highlight for the ages. They were so proud to be included and to help spread the message they did.

In a single moment, I learned the power of emotion and how it can change people. Abigail transcended her emotions like no one I've ever met and made everyone around her feel the surge of energy that she was releasing. I want to be around more people like that, and I'll do my best to never forget what she said: "Nothing is prettier than happy!"

MAKING IT MATTER

Essence of the Moment

Happiness is contagious, and when someone radiates pure joy, it has the power to uplift everyone around them. Abigail's unfiltered excitement was a beautiful reminder that being happy is one of life's most magnetic and transformative states.

Timeless Truths

☑ **Happiness Amplifies Connection:** Joy has a unique ability to draw people together, creating shared moments that linger long after they pass.

☑ **Recognition Elevates Worth:** Acknowledging someone's value or qualities can spark pride and gratitude in ways that words alone can't express.

☑ **Emotion Creates Ripples:** The energy we put into the world doesn't just stay with us—it impacts everyone we encounter.

Bringing It Home

1. **Celebrate Someone's Joy:** Think about someone who's radiated happiness recently. Send them a quick message or give them a heartfelt compliment today to let them know how much their energy means to you.
2. **Focus on What Brings You Happiness:** Set aside time this week to do something that fills you with joy—whether it's a favorite activity, connecting with someone uplifting, or simply slowing down to enjoy a moment.
3. **Create a Moment of Recognition:** Over the next few weeks, plan a meaningful way to show appreciation to someone who inspires you. It could be a thoughtful note, a small gift, or just telling them how much they matter.

Next Level Thinking

Ask yourself:
- How often do I intentionally recognize and celebrate the joy or achievements of others?
- What small changes can I make to prioritize and amplify happiness in my daily life?
- Who in my life consistently radiates positivity, and how can I show them appreciation?
- How can I create opportunities to spread joy and connection in my community or personal circles?

Insight to Remember

"Nothing is prettier than happy!"
- Abigail Milby

18

THE POWER OF BELIEF

Deep into the fourth inning, something magical happened. And when it did, everything stopped. It was an unexpected moment that took everyone's breath away.

Eight weeks prior, I was welcoming my new Little League team. There was Caleb, John, Garrett, Chris, and a number of other boys—and then there was my two: McKenzie and Breanna.

They had learned baseball with me and wanted to play baseball—not softball. They were quick, knew how to throw, could catch, and were strong hitters—especially for nine and ten-year-olds.

Our team was special. We didn't have anyone that had ever pitched before, nor did we have any catchers. Several had never played baseball at all, some didn't know how to run, and some didn't speak any English. We had our challenges, to say the least.

It was literally like a modern-day Bad News Bears team.

We practiced... a lot. In a three-week period, we had the makings of what looked like an actual team. A week later, we played our first game and got beat, but put up a great fight. At the end of the game, we gathered up in the outfield and I went over everything that went right—lots of high-fives and celebrations, even in defeat.

By the end of the third game, every single player on the team had gotten at least one hit—except one. Some players already had as many as five; some had triples, and a few had doubles. That one player, though, had made good contact several times but never made it to base.

That player was Breanna.

We worked hard outside of practice. Training tools were deployed. Timing devices, tees for contact, batting cages—all of it. Breanna was doing well in practice, but it just didn't pan out in the games.

Game four—same result. Two walks and a pop-out. She came really close though, several times with foul balls, but she just couldn't connect when she needed to—and where she needed to.

"I almost got on base, Dad!" she told me afterward with a disappointed smile that told me she was taking it hard.

We got to a point where all the guys on the team were cheering her on. I mean, she was likable and worked hard, but she just couldn't catch a break. Every time she'd go up to bat—another disappointment. Game five came and went. Game six—up and gone. Seven and eight—same thing.

"I'm gonna get a hit, Dad—you just watch!"

Practices were fun. Everyone was getting better and more confident, including Breanna. Prior to game nine, she asked if she could be the "batter" and hit over and over to provide infield practice for the team. She was there batting for close to an hour and was hitting them left and right—literally.

She was resilient and ready to put this behind her. The team believed in her. Her family and friends believed in her. I believed in her. But more importantly, she believed in herself.

Game nine comes, and her first at-bat results in a walk. Her second at-bat is a grounder, where she gets thrown out. Third at-bat, and she looks determined.

Mind you, the entire team and crowd is cheering for her. This is now a big deal—to them, to her, to everyone. As our team was batting, I was the third-base coach, watching everything from straight down the line.

Strike one—she takes a pitch down the middle and swings like she was aiming for the fences, but missed. Next pitch: straight down the middle again, and she foul-tips it off behind her. I'm there clapping with encouragement and telling her, "Good eye, good eye," and, "Hang in there!"

The next pitch was just like the others: solid and straight down the middle. This time, though, Breanna connected with the sweetest sound a player could hear and hit a line drive up over the shortstop's head and into the outfield. The crowd is going wild, she's running and jumping with excitement on her way to first, and I'm nearly having a heart attack watching it all unfold.

As quickly as I could, I got the umpire's attention and called for a time-out on the field. He called "TIME," and I immediately started running over to Breanna, with my arms outstretched, while exclaiming, "YEAAAAAAAHHHHH!"

The game had stopped, but the cheers were still coming—from her friends, the team, the crowd, her family—and me.

When I got to her, she jumped into my arms, and we spun around with me saying, "You did it! You did it!" over and over—right there at first base. If it had been a movie, fireworks would have gone off right then.

The celebration probably lasted ten seconds or less, but that moment will forever live rent-free in my mind. Because it wasn't just a hit—it was a milestone. Breanna could have given up at any point, but she didn't. She could have said that baseball isn't for her, but it never happened. Day after day, she showed up, worked hard, and delivered in the face of adversity.

"THAT WAS AWESOME!!!" she said after the game while her teammates celebrated with her. Not only did she feel like she belonged, but that she was a contributor to the team—and that, my friends, is important.

Confidence is built from moments like this: personally, as an athlete, and as a human. Sometimes, it takes a little longer for fruit to ripen, but that just makes it that much sweeter when it does.

My girl didn't just get a hit—she overcame a major challenge. One she'll carry with her the rest of her days. And I'm so proud to have been there the day it happened and to see the joy only a moment like that can provide.

MAKING IT MATTER

Essence of the Moment

Believing in yourself and having others believe in you can create life-changing moments. Breanna's persistence and determination remind us that growth often comes from pushing through challenges—and the joy of finally succeeding is unparalleled.

Timeless Truths

☑ **Perseverance Pays Off:** Staying committed through setbacks leads to victories that build lasting confidence.

☑ **Support Fuels Success:** Encouragement from others creates a foundation for personal growth and achievement.

☑ **Celebrate Every Win:** Recognizing milestones, no matter how small, strengthens self-belief and motivation.

Bringing It Home

1. **Encourage Someone's Effort:** Take a moment today to encourage someone working hard at something, whether they're succeeding yet or not. A little belief can go a long way.
2. **Push Through Your Own Challenges:** This week, focus on one area where you've been struggling. Commit to showing up and giving it your all, even if success feels far away.
3. **Celebrate a Recent Milestone:** Reflect on a personal or shared win this month. Share the joy with someone who was part of your journey or helped you along the way.

Next Level Thinking

Ask yourself:

▷ How do I respond to setbacks in my own life, and what can I learn from Breanna's determination?

▷ Who has believed in me during a difficult time, and how can I show gratitude for their support?

▷ How can I create an environment where others feel encouraged to persevere?

▷ What small steps can I take today to build confidence in myself or someone else?

Insight to Remember

"Confidence is built from moments like this: personally, as an athlete, and as a human. Sometimes it takes a little longer for fruit to ripen, but that just makes it that much sweeter when it does."

19

A NEW NORM

January 1st.

A day marked both by celebration and a poignant history that spanned over four decades. It was her anniversary. Well, their anniversary. And it wasn't just her routine—it was her "Norm."

The last fifteen years have been a struggle, marked by the relentless toll Parkinson's can take on loved ones. Changes unfolded, conversations shifted, abilities waned, and friendships evolved, altering the very fabric of her life. Of their life.

This last year was different.

Now, as a widow, an inquisitive traveler, a worn mother, and the sole decision-maker in an unfamiliar town in Kansas, new chaos was unfolding. Emotions of anger, betrayal, and desertion enveloped her.

But then, something changed.

And this, friends, is a story about vulnerability, compassion, and the beauty of letting new experiences in. Specifically, it's about a lady who found solace, laughter, wonder, and connection in an unexpected place. For her, it was a chance to see the world through a different lens and to find the good. It opened her eyes to the little things all around and gave her a new perspective.

She was one of the first people to tell me she'd read my book, cover to cover. And that she was going to share it with everyone she met. And that it resonated in such a positive way that she was going to post a glowing review for it.

She's a lady of her word and did what she said she would.

"Norm" was her husband and her best friend until he passed. He was an adrenaline junkie and her knight in shining armor. They did everything together and traveled frequently. They were into several sports, and she was his biggest supporter. They raised children together and made a life work... until it didn't.

Times change, and so do people. People harden over time if left to their own vices. Walls close in and have a way of making us all feel like there won't be a happy ending.

But, as this lady would soon find out, nothing is as it seems. You can lose twenty hands in a row and then get blackjack. That's kind of how this next situation turned out.

Over about four months, I had several hundred interactions with this lady. On posts, through email, in Messenger, and in a group we're in. She was a huge advocate for the book, had ordered more copies than anyone, and always wanted them signed.

She said she used them as a starting point for conversations and that she'd read out different chapters to groups of ladies she was a part of. Her favorite is Chapter 11: The WAP. She says it gets people laughing, AND they love how it ends up having a life lesson with it.

So, in November, we talked, and she told me a bit more about her story—specifically, about January 1st—and how she was dreading it. Mind you, it was just a conversation, and she wasn't asking for anything.

It wasn't the first time she'd told me. Nor the second. I reached a point where I'd connected the dots and figured it out. It wasn't that she was complaining, but that she was hurting.

"Why don't you come spend the holidays with us?" I asked.

No, she's not family. No, we'd never met. No, I hadn't asked anyone else for permission. No, I didn't have any ulterior motives. No, I didn't know if she was a serial killer. No, I didn't think she'd accept.

"Are you serious?" she inquired.

I explained that we always have a big party for New Year's,

and she could join right in with our family. This way, she wouldn't have to be alone. She wouldn't drown in sorrow. And she could meet some of the people she'd read about in the book.

I'm sure many people thought she was crazy. She didn't care. Some even told her she was. Didn't matter. Sometimes you have to take a chance, and take a chance she did.

The next day, she told me she'd booked flights, rented a car, and requested time off of work and was going to make it happen.

She was thrilled.

Fast forward to the day we met. It was the 30th of December. She called and said she was in a Dollar General parking lot just a few miles from our house. She was tired from more than twelve hours of traveling, so I told her to hang tight and that we'd be there in a couple of minutes.

Five minutes later, we showed up, and I knew I'd made the right decision. It was a surreal moment. She was standing by her car, waving, with the most heartfelt smile you could imagine and a shirt with the perfect message, "BE GOOD TO PEOPLE."

My wife and I got out of the car, and it felt like we were reuniting with a long-lost friend. After a couple of long hugs, I asked if I could drive her car the rest of the way in so she could take in the sights. She agreed, and we were off.

The next five days were filled with conversation, laughter, tears, food, drinks, music, meeting people, blackjack, touring the area, and taking in more than I could ever write about.

She met Mr. Bobby, Grandma Mary, and many other "characters." Perhaps my favorite moment of all was when she left Amon's and walked towards the car. She had a box of goodies, a smile, and a pep in her step like no other.

She was glowing!

She got in the car and was thrilled to have seen it for herself, met the owner, discussed the book, and helped support their business.

When she arrived, she had a lot of baggage. Some I could carry for her, and the rest was in her head. We all have baggage like that.

Somehow, when she left, it was like she'd sorted through it all and was ready to leave some big pieces behind. Even then, I'm certain she left with much more than she came with... but it was in the form of a full heart and memories that won't soon fade.

She told me about all the people she'd met at the airport, on the plane, and on her way back home and how excited they were to hear of her experience. She even gave three strangers signed books and would have given out more if she'd had them.

We rarely get to hear what our words actually mean to someone. We rarely get to see that it truly inspires and changes someone. We rarely get to see a real-life transformation take place in front of our eyes.

But I saw it.

And it was beautiful, deep, and meaningful. To her. To us. To me.

Sharon, thank you for being the you you've always wanted to be. I hope your life continues to get better and better and that it becomes your new "Norm."

Just remember—it's your story, and YOU get to choose what characters are in it, how you tell it, what you reveal... and when.

Make it a good one!

MAKING IT MATTER

Essence of the Moment

When we take a chance on connection, we create opportunities for transformation—not just for others, but for ourselves. Sharon's journey shows us how shared experiences and kindness can help turn life's challenges into meaningful new beginnings.

Timeless Truths

- ☑ **Kindness Can Transform:** Offering someone a lifeline can bring joy, healing, and hope when they need it most.
- ☑ **Courage Changes Lives:** Taking risks—whether by extending an invitation or saying yes to one—opens doors to unexpected joy.
- ☑ **Baggage Can Be Lifted:** Letting go of past hurts allows space for new experiences and connections to thrive.

Bringing It Home

1. **Reach Out to Someone:** Think about someone who might be struggling right now. Send them a message or make a call today to let them know they're not alone.
2. **Create Space for Connection:** Invite someone into your world this week—a coffee date, a phone call, or even a shopping trip. Each has the potential of a shared moment of laughter that can make a difference.
3. **Take a Leap of Faith:** Say "yes" to something by the end of the month that feels a little outside your comfort zone. You never know what new chapters it might write in your story.

Next Level Thinking

Ask yourself:

▷ How can I create opportunities for meaningful connection with those who might be feeling isolated?

▷ When have I taken a leap of faith that changed the trajectory of my life, and what can I learn from that?

▷ Who has extended kindness to me in my toughest moments, and how can I pay it forward?

▷ What am I still carrying that I need to let go of to create space for new experiences?

Insight to Remember

"It's your story, and YOU get to choose what characters are in it, how you tell it, what you reveal... and when."

20

THE CROSSROADS

We were at the proverbial crossroads: keep going and burn out, go left and lose everything we'd invested, or go right and build something entirely new.

It was late in the evening. The air had started to cool, but our conversation was heating up. It was just me, Joanna, and a baby stroller with our four-month-old daughter, trying to decide how to proceed.

Two years earlier, I had left a job I loved to create the company we were discussing. Three months after leaving, I took a new job to help fund it, working long hours during the day and building the business after hours. Literal blood, sweat, tears—and tens of thousands of dollars—had gone into what we'd built.

Now, it was all at risk.

"You can't keep doing this to your family—they deserve better," one of my relatives had told me. "It's not working—you need to just go back to your day job," another had said, disappointment heavy in her voice. "Why can't you just be okay with what you have?"

Joanna had heard all the comments, and the weight was getting to her.

She was exhausted. I was exhausted. We all were.

When we started the company, it revolved around teaching people to dance in a single weekend. And it worked—beautifully!

We'd created 4-hour, 8-hour, and 16-hour seminars using a sports-based curriculum I had developed.

Our success came at a price. Every weekend, we were on the road, either promoting events or hosting them.

Now, with a newborn, the pace became unsustainable. Joanna wanted to be home with our daughter—and wanted me there, too.

This particular conversation was in early November. I remember Joanna saying, "I'll keep helping until the New Year, but after that, I'm done."

I didn't blame her. The strain had reached a breaking point, and I had to decide.

"All I need to do is find a way to replicate myself..." I said, half-cocked, clinging to hope. "There just has to be a way!" Mind you, I'd hired and trained some ten instructors that year, but it wasn't the same. People didn't come for "a class"—I was told, repeatedly, they came for the way I taught it.

Still, it felt like everyone I knew—including Joanna—was telling me to give it up.

For the better part of the next week, I lost sleep. My mind wouldn't let this one go as I felt like I was so close, but I couldn't figure it out.

Then, a lightbulb moment happened.

Without telling anyone but one of my employees, I rented an event hall, set up a backdrop, and placed a camera on a tripod. How hard could it be to do an instructional video?

We spent the day filming lesson after lesson until I was satisfied. It wasn't glamorous—I had to stop and start constantly, fumbling with my lines and the setup—but we had something to go on.

The next day, I bought editing software and got to work. I would soon discover that we knew nothing about lighting, sound, or camera angles. With editing and all sorts of cuts, trims, transitions, and fades, my video turned into an absolute mess.

"This is awful!" I blurted during the first viewing. "We have to figure this out."

Determined, I shifted focus. I mocked up DVD covers in Photoshop, set up a website, and created listings for products I didn't yet have. A week later, I ran an ad for my nonexistent DVDs.

It worked!

Orders started coming in, and over a three-week period, we pre-sold almost fifty DVDs. Fifty DVDs we hadn't even made. Now what?

Time was running out. Joanna's deadline was looming, and customers were inquiring about their orders. Driving home from work one Friday afternoon, I noticed a small billboard in a rundown neighborhood: "Dan's Video and DVD Service."

I called immediately, and within fifteen minutes, I was at Dan's doorstep. An hour later, a plan.

By Sunday morning, we had rented a studio and arranged a small film crew, and we were ready.

Aaaannnnnnnd.... Action!

Six hours later, we'd filmed three complete lessons—one for each of the DVDs we'd pre-sold. With only two HD cameras, Dan assured me it would only take a few hours. Dan and I started at six that evening, and I ended up staying around the clock, editing furiously.

By 6am, the DVDs were done. Two days later, every pre-order was shipped—with two days to spare.

I had figured out how to replicate myself—how to teach every weekend without being gone.

Oh, those first three DVDs weren't pretty—at all, but they were full of lessons. Not as many for the people buying them, but TONS for me. They gave me a chance to catch my breath at a time when I was gasping for air.

Over the next eight years, we would create nearly seventy-five full-length instructional DVDs, selling in over 130 countries. That moment—standing at the crossroads—had set the stage for a future I couldn't have imagined. We then spent the next five years converting all our lessons to the digital platform that we have now.

And it wasn't just about saving my business—it was about saving my family, my weekends, and, ultimately, my purpose.

Looking back, I realize that moment was transformative—not just for my career but my life. It taught me the value of innovation under pressure, the importance of adaptability, and the incredible power of believing in a vision when no one else does.

Sometimes, the most difficult decisions in life are the ones that lead to the most profound changes. It's in those moments of crisis that clarity emerges. And for me, that clarity came with a camera, a DVD cover, and a dream I wouldn't let die.

MAKING IT MATTER

Essence of the Moment

Moments of crisis can feel like dead ends, but they're often the turning points that lead to reinvention. By choosing to adapt rather than quit, I found a way to save not just my business but my family and my purpose.

Timeless Truths

- ☑ **Adaptation Sparks Survival:** When faced with adversity, finding new ways to approach challenges can turn setbacks into breakthroughs.
- ☑ **Pressure Fuels Innovation:** Necessity can inspire creativity and lead to solutions you never imagined.
- ☑ **Belief Drives Change:** Even when others doubt, unwavering faith in your vision can pave the way forward.

Bringing It Home

1. **Explore New Avenues:** Think of one area where you're stuck today. Spend time brainstorming or researching a creative solution you haven't tried before.

2. **Create Meaningful Momentum:** Take a meaningful first step this week. One that moves in the direction of an idea you've been hesitant to act on. Even small progress can create lasting momentum.
3. **Reflect and Reimagine:** By the end of this month, assess a challenge in your life and identify how adapting your approach could lead to a breakthrough.

Next Level Thinking

Ask yourself:
▷ How do I typically respond to moments of crises—do I freeze, fight, or adapt?
▷ What is one area of my life where I need to rethink my approach to create a different outcome?
▷ Who has shown belief in me when I've doubted myself, and how can I honor or learn from their faith?
▷ What's one risk I'm willing to take to ensure I'm aligned with my purpose and vision?

Insight to Remember

"Sometimes, the hardest decisions in life are the ones that lead to the most profound changes. It's in those moments of crisis that clarity emerges."

21

THE PROBLEM IS...

Two women were manning the fort.

By fort, I mean hotel.

By manning, I mean just kind of existing.

One was on her phone, and the other talked to a friend while guests waited.

The problem is that they were the only two people working at the front desk of an Embassy Suites in Nashville, and the line was at least five guests deep.

Thirty-five minutes of waiting and I abort. Three hours later, I deliver. This time, it's to a manager named Houston.

"Houston, we have a problem..." I started with once I learned his name. He smiled. I smiled. It was on.

Houston's from Chicago, loves New Orleans, and lives in Nashville.

He and I are so incredibly different, yet we're strangely alike. He listens to my story and asks questions. He empathizes and takes notes. He vows to make changes immediately... and he does.

This moment happened some fifteen years ago, and we've been friends ever since. We often go out of our way to see him while we're traveling, and he happens to be our most frequent guest at our house. He's now part of our family and often tells people he and I are brothers.

Houston has an MBA, and so do I. We went to different schools together. We grew up in dissimilar neighborhoods at the same time and have experienced the world together, differently, for the same amount of time—we're the same age, so our birthdays practically make us twins.

Houston's a wealth of information, a historian, is uber professional, and the storyteller of storytellers. He cracks me up with some of his messages and often sends me cryptic texts. Past that, he's wildly entertaining and has a large presence that often affords him more ear time than most. It's a gift of his, and his ability to either recall or make things up on the spot is uncannily uncanny.

The more I get to know Houston, the more I see how different we are, and I love it. Why? Because it strengthens our relationship. I'll never live the life he lives, and I'll never see the world through his eyes, but it's an important perspective I can't get without him. We talk through current events, and I see and pick up on the little things he connects with, and I register his thoughts and feelings as they relate.

And, by the way, I listen to Houston and his perspective, as it's a valuable piece of the puzzle I'm constantly putting together. I'd never claim to understand what it's like to be black like he is, but, for the record, I'd never claim to understand what it's like to be white. And that's because we're ALL different. I've said this before, but stereotyping is ridiculous. Like, I can't tell you a thing about what "white people" think or do as there's no two of us that are the same —heck, even in my own family, there's very little you'd be able to glean from any one of us as our lives are all so drastically different, yet we co-exist.

We co-exist as humans and have to navigate this crazy world together. Black, white, brown, gay, straight, democrat, republican, male, female, independent, skinny, fat, fit, whatever... they're all just attributes, but they don't describe us—they divide us, period. Maybe the "period" is what the problem is. Without the period, our nation's acronym of the U.S. would just be US—and that's exactly what we need again.

I'm writing about Houston because he's got the heart of a servant and treats US as though we not only matter but are part of

HIS family, and he helps take care of us. He's part of "my people," and I'm part of his.

His background and daily life fascinate me, and mine's the same to him. We talk regularly and for hours at a time. I tell stories—he tells stories—we both listen, and we both learn. We both help each other, and we both laugh at each other. He does and thinks some strange crap, and I call him out on it, and vice versa. I tell him about the randomness I get into, and he laughs and often raises his drink to mine.

It just is.

Today, I'd like to share my appreciation for moments that create friendships and friendships that make us better people. Friendships that challenge us to be better than we were yesterday. Friendships that allow us to listen to and appreciate different perspectives. Friendships that bridge the gap of cultural, societal, and racial differences and allow us all to be ourselves. Friendships that are okay with being completely different humans and enjoying each other for our hearts and minds.

Friends, if you don't have someone like Houston in your life, get one. Get yourself someone you can laugh with, hang with, send crazy memes to, talk to, listen to, have drinks with, go to clubs with, watch movies with, talk tiki torches with, explore music with, close down pubs with, and cry with.

We all need each other, and we need to have each other's backs. Houston, I've got yours, and thanks for getting mine.

Oh, and, Houston, we no longer have a problem!

MAKING IT MATTER

Essence of the Moment

True friendships thrive on differences, challenging us to grow while appreciating the beauty in shared humanity. Building connections that transcend labels creates bridges that make life richer and more meaningful.

Timeless Truths

☑ **Friendships Transcend Differences:** Real connections are built by embracing what makes us unique while finding common ground.

☑ **Listening Builds Bridges:** Genuine listening fosters understanding and strengthens relationships across all divides.

☑ **Unity Through Humanity:** When we focus on what connects us instead of what separates us, we create a stronger, more inclusive community.

Bringing It Home

1. **Prioritize Listening:** The next time you're in a conversation, maybe even today, pause to let someone else lead. Ask open-ended questions, listen deeply, and take note of the insights they share.
2. **Expand Your Circle:** This week, look for opportunities to connect with someone new. A colleague, neighbor, or community member might offer a fresh perspective that could spark a valuable new friendship.
3. **Reach Out and Reflect:** Before the month ends, take stock of the diversity in your friendships. Think about the stories, perspectives, and experiences they've shared with you, and send a note of appreciation to someone who's impacted your life.

Next Level Thinking

Ask yourself:
- How can I build relationships that embrace differences and encourage mutual growth?
- Do I take time to truly listen to others, or do I focus more on sharing my perspective?
- What steps can I take to foster understanding and empathy in my personal and professional interactions?
- How can I celebrate and amplify the unique voices in my community to create a more inclusive environment?

Insight to Remember

"Today, I'd like to share my appreciation for moments that create friendships and friendships that make us better people."

22

I'VE GOT THIS

We barely slept—an hour, maybe two, at most. We couldn't—our minds were all but crippled by the conversation we'd had near midnight the night before.

The chaplain's voice echoed in our heads. "You should prepare for the worst."

Our daughter, whom we'd not yet held, wasn't doing well, and the challenges just kept piling up. Pneumonia. Oxygen levels. A breathing machine. Each day brought her new hurdles, and now, this.

6am rolled around, and we were back, deep breaths and all, waiting to get buzzed into the hospital. Armed with coffees that were still steaming, we got in and zombie-walked our way to the elevators.

The elevator opened, and just as we were about to step in, the charge nurse stepped out.

"Breanna's your daughter, right?" the charge nurse asked, with an emotionless face I couldn't read.

"Uh... yes," I said with a very uneasy feeling where my eyes bulged and my heart started racing.

"Did they call and tell you what happened?" the charge nurse asked.

There are moments in life that freeze time. When your body betrays you—your chest tightens, your skin goes cold, and you forget how to breathe.

This was one of those moments.

I was sure we were about to hear the words no parent wants to hear—that our baby girl didn't make it through the night. That the tiny glimmer of hope we were clinging to was extinguished. That we'd never get the chance to hold and hug her while she was alive.

For context, Breanna was a six-week preemie, born just ten days earlier. Within minutes of being born, she'd been rushed to the NICU, sealed off in her own little "bubble."

Her first days were a blur. Tubes, wires, and nodes—each one a lifeline. She struggled to breathe and battled pneumonia. Machines pumped air into her tiny little lungs that weren't quite ready for the world.

And all we could do was watch her from a distance.

Every step forward came with three steps back. Optimism wasn't high among her caretakers, and the cold reality of how fragile life can be was starting to get the best of them.

But our hopes were high, and our prayers went higher.

So, with my heart still racing, I answered her question. "No ma'am, we haven't heard anything. What's going on?"

In the middle of my fear, she smiled. It felt jarring, almost cruel —until she spoke. "She pulled all her tubes out just before three this morning," the nurse said, nearly laughing with excitement. "And she's breathing on her own."

We stared at her, uncomprehending. Her words hung in the air like they were a different language. *Breathing on her own*? Four words that sounded too good to be true.

"She's quite the fighter!" she says with a big toothy smile while nodding in the affirmative. "It was like a switch was flipped, and she was ready to do it all on her own."

I slow-blinked, took a breath, and restarted my heart... all at the same time. And so did Joanna.

The elevator ride felt endless. Neither of us spoke. We didn't dare. My hands tightened around the coffee cup, now cold, and I kept my eyes fixed on the numbers lighting up beside the door.

What waited for us on the other side? Hope? Heartbreak?

When the doors opened, the silence was deafening. It remained until we found her station.

And what we saw was the most beautiful little girl with nothing but a single heart monitor on her wrist. Her tiny chest rose and fell steadily. No wires. No tubes. Just her.

After getting the "go-ahead," I reached out tentatively, my fingers brushing against her soft skin. She was warm. Alive. Our very own miracle baby right there in front of us.

Moments later, they handed her to us for the first time. I'd thought about this moment since the day she was born, but nothing could prepare me for how it felt to hold her in my arms.

It felt like a dream that I didn't want to wake from.

Two days later, we brought her home. The drive felt surreal—almost like we were carrying something too precious for the world.

That was the story of how Breanna literally just flipped the switch when she was ready and did things on her terms. Little did we know her childhood would repeat that same pattern over and over.

A set of qualities that would serve her well and allow her to make a positive impact in everything she was a part of. Now, as a young adult, she's working her way through college and continues to excel in athletics, academics, and personal wellness.

Breanna's entrance, though, was extraordinary. She taught us something no doctor, nurse, or textbook ever could: no matter how impossible the odds, the human spirit is limitless. That love, hope, and resilience can move mountains.

Breanna's fight reminded us that every breath is a gift. That the smallest victories are often the most incredible miracles. And that sometimes, when you think all is lost, you've got to pull out all your lifelines, flip a switch, and just say, "I've got this."

MAKING IT MATTER

Essence of the Moment

The power of resilience is extraordinary. Breanna's story reminds us that strength lies within, and sometimes, you just have to trust yourself and say, "I've got this."

Timeless Truths

- ☑ **Inner Strength Wins Battles:** When faced with overwhelming odds, the will to fight can defy even the toughest challenges.
- ☑ **Hope Fuels Miracles:** Holding onto hope can open the door to unexpected triumphs.
- ☑ **Celebrate Small Victories:** Even the tiniest steps forward can bring life-changing moments of joy.

Bringing It Home

1. **Trust Your Inner Strength:** Think about a challenge you're facing. Today, remind yourself of your own resilience and take one small step forward.
2. **Focus on the Positive:** Keep track of even the smallest victories in your life this week. Write them down and celebrate the progress you've made.
3. **Inspire Hope in Others:** Before the month ends, share a story of overcoming challenges with someone who might need encouragement. Your words could help spark their belief in themselves.

Ask yourself:

- When faced with overwhelming challenges, how do I remind myself of my inner strength and resilience?
- How can I better appreciate the small victories in my life that signify progress?
- Who in my life has shown extraordinary perseverance, and what can I learn from their example?
- In what ways can I channel difficult moments into opportunities for growth and self-discovery?

Insight to Remember

"Breanna's fight reminded us that every breath is a gift. That the smallest victories are often the most incredible miracles."

23

INSPIRATION

He pointed at me and said, "You're on MY team."
Sure, it was just a pick-up basketball game, but there was more to it.

Every single time he was captain, he'd pick me for his team. And vice-versa. We worked well together. We supported one another and made things happen for others. He had an incredible amount of energy and was always talking crap to the other team in a good way.

It was entertaining, to say the least, and we both always felt like we had a chance as long as there was still time left.

That was in high school, and we've since gone our separate ways. Like, everything about our lives was different.

Except who we were then and how we made each other feel. Mutual respect is just that.

His name is Josh, and last week I called him. I wanted him to know I was thinking of him and to thank him for inspiring me.

Josh has been through so much in his life and has seen what most of us don't want to. Josh has two Purple Hearts and stories that'll make the hair on your skin stand at attention.

When Josh answered the phone, he said, in his best motivational voice, "TRAUTMAN, YOU GLORIOUS MOTHERF%^*+*^!"

Josh doesn't just talk his game—he plays it. Josh is all about helping his community, building people up, and fighting for what's right for humanity.

A week after our talk, I saw a post from him and wanted to share his message... and ironically, it was from a note he wrote to himself back in 2019. In it, he says:

Master
Yourself
Master
Everything

Friends, listen: those four words, when written together, can stand the test of time.

Appropriately, he wrote them on top of one another, allowing us to "read between the lines."

Those words can relate to our actions, our responses, our feelings, and our goals. It can also relate to our food, our sleep, our exercise, and our habits.

If we master ourselves, the influence of marketing, corrupt leaders, and mass media will disappear. We get to choose how our days go, who we interact with, and what we get involved in.

It's a goal, not a destination, and he knows it. He lives it. He struggles on the daily, but keeps pushing forward. He does his best to not let his emotions get the best of him, but he's still human. He actively pushes for greatness all around him and then falls at the end of each day and feels like giving up.

But he doesn't, and that's inspiring to me. He has strong convictions, and they are also inspiring to me. He has a "do anything it takes" attitude like most Marines I know, and that, too, is inspiring to me.

And he regularly tells me how much I motivate and inspire him. Just like when we were playing ball.

Josh, thanks for being you and for allowing me to be me. Turns out, "You're on MY team" is a lifetime appointment, and guess what? There's still time left on the clock—we still have a chance! Oorah!

MAKING IT MATTER

True inspiration comes from those who push through struggles, stand firm in their convictions, and uplift those around them. Josh's story reminds us of the power of perseverance, camaraderie, and the lasting impact of shared respect.

Timeless Truths

- ☑ **Master Yourself First:** Personal discipline is the foundation for facing life's challenges with strength and resilience.
- ☑ **Respect Builds Bonds:** Mutual respect creates unbreakable connections that stand the test of time.
- ☑ **Inspiration is Contagious:** By striving for greatness, we not only improve ourselves but also motivate others to rise.

Bringing It Home

1. **Start With Yourself:** Think about one area of your life where you can build more discipline. Today, take a single step to master it—whether it's your mindset, habits, or emotions.
2. **Rekindle Old Connections:** Reach out this week to someone from your past who inspired or motivated you. Let them know their impact on your life.
3. **Be Someone's Team Captain:** Before the month ends, identify someone who could use support or encouragement and actively be a source of positivity for them.

Next Level Thinking

Ask yourself:
- ▷ How often do I stop to truly appreciate the friendships and connections that shape my life?

- What can I do today to show gratitude for someone who has inspired or supported me?
- How am I fostering relationships that challenge and strengthen me in meaningful ways?
- How can I be more intentional about surrounding myself with people who uplift and motivate me?

Insight to Remember

"If we master ourselves, the influence of marketing, corrupt leaders, and mass media will disappear. We get to choose how our days go, who we interact with, and what we get involved in."

24

A LIFE WORTH PURSUING

Just as the rock I'd kicked tumbled down the secluded one-lane road, I asked, "Wouldn't it be great if life came with a cheat sheet?" Joanna looked at me, half-amused, half-annoyed—you know, like usual.

"Why? So you could tell me what happens next?" she shot back, smirking like only she can do.

To our right was a stocked catfish pond with the moon's reflection perfectly settled into the middle. Strangely, there was an immense calm—not a ripple in sight. Quite different than the turbulence I knew she was feeling inside.

"Nope," I said, slowing my steps to an almost stop. "It's so you could tell me what you really want out of life."

She laughed the kind of laugh that says, *You can't be serious*.

"What do you mean? I don't know... survive?"

But I wasn't letting her off the hook that easily.

I pressed. She pushed back. I pressed harder. Her steps slowed.

She stared at the water and pondered. "I mean, I guess I'd want to... well, you know. Help people." Her voice tapered off as if she didn't fully believe it. Because she didn't.

We stood there, talking, as darkness settled in. About dreams, fears, possibilities, and what comes next with kids moving on. By the time we started our slow ascent home, I could tell her wheels were spinning, but I didn't know where they were going. Nor did she.

For the next four weeks, I made sure her plate was cleared so she could do some deep thinking. Soul-searching, if you will. Golf tournaments, family excursions, and road trips kept me and the kids out of her hair, giving her the space to explore the question most never get to explore.

And explore she did.

Then, out of the blue one evening, it happened. "I want to help people!" she said, and as her words hung in the air from the built-in tension, I waited. "And I know what I have to do," she said through a smile. A real smile, not the polite or passive kind, but the kind where you know someone's got it figured out. A real-life awakening.

That moment changed everything. Within days, Joanna enrolled online at a university to pursue a secondary bachelor's degree in dietetics. Her passion for food, chemistry, and public health was in a blender, and she was well on her way.

Shortly after diving into her coursework, Joanna realized she didn't need to wait to start helping people. She could begin sharing her knowledge immediately if she were to start her own YouTube channel.

Two weeks later, Joanna stood in our kitchen, nervously rehearsing her intro. Our cats gathered around her like an impromptu audience filled with silent stares and ear-piercing meows that were both curious and amusing. Her hands were trembling, her voice was shaky, and the camera was rolling as she introduced herself to an audience she didn't yet have. "Hi, I'm Joanna Trautman. Welcome to How to Really Cook!"

With each take, her confidence grew. Her voice steadied, her smile brightened, and her mission became more apparent.

Comments started rolling in... by the thousands. 'I never thought I'd be able to make something so healthy,' one person wrote. Another said, 'Your videos have completely changed the way I think about what I feed my pets,' And then this one, 'Watching your videos has inspired me to be more intentional, not just with my pets' health, but with how I approach nutrition for my whole family. You're helping more than you know.'

Every new comment on her channel made her feel like she was taking a victory lap. She'd read them aloud with a grin as if each brought her one step closer to her dream.

But her journey wasn't without pain. A year and a half later and one semester away from graduation, something changed. New restrictions on masks and in-person classes were put in place, and her plans were derailed. "I'm not doing it," she said, angrily shaking her head. "It'll just have to wait."

She could have given up, but she didn't. Instead of quitting, she shifted her focus to a Master's degree and started teaching Biology, where she found a whole new way to impact people's lives. Now, she's enrolled in a second Master's program, teaching, inspiring, building her channel, and has shifted her dreams of becoming a registered dietician due to new AI-leveraged technology that she believes will reshape that industry in the upcoming years.

Looking back, I realize how many lives were changed that night by the pond. Mine, hers, our kids, those who've seen her videos, and those in the schools.

That walk was really just her stepping into her calling. She just needed me to hold the mirror so she could see the true reflection of her inner self.

They say walks can clear your mind, but I say they can change your life. Joanna's journey isn't just about where she's going—it's about the path she's carving for others to follow.

MAKING IT MATTER

Essence of the Moment

Finding your purpose doesn't happen overnight, but when you uncover what truly drives you, it creates a ripple effect that transforms not only your life but also the lives of those you touch.

Timeless Truths

☑ **Clarity Sparks Courage:** Discovering what truly matters gives you the strength to take bold steps forward.
☑ **Purpose Evolves with Action:** Sometimes, the journey of pursuing what you love uncovers new opportunities you didn't expect.
☑ **Guidance Builds Momentum:** A thoughtful question or conversation can set someone on a path they were meant to take.

Bringing It Home

1. **Take a Reflective Walk:** Dedicate time today for a quiet walk or moment of reflection. Ask yourself, "What would I do if I could do anything?" Let the answers surface without judgment.
2. **Identify One Small Action:** This week, take a single step toward something you've been dreaming about—it could be researching a new career path, starting a project, or exploring a passion.
3. **Be Someone's Mirror:** Encourage someone who may need help discovering their own potential. See if you can do it before the month ends. Sometimes, all it takes is a nudge to make a life-changing difference.

Next Level Thinking

Ask yourself:

- ▷ What do I truly want to pursue, and how can I take one step toward it today?
- ▷ How can I create space for someone else to discover their own purpose or passion?
- ▷ What fears or doubts might be holding me back from fully embracing my potential?
- ▷ How can I adapt and grow when life's challenges disrupt my plans?

Insight to Remember

"That walk was really just her stepping into her calling. She just needed me to hold the mirror so she could see the true reflection of her inner self."

25

MAKING THE CUT

Words can't describe my feelings in that moment. For weeks, I'd gone door-to-door raising money for the church, and now, I was reaping the benefits. The reward was all mine.

Well, there were three of us. And our fathers. The top three fundraisers were to get tickets to the game. Buccaneers versus the Bears—always one of the season's best games, and we were ready!

Dressed in everything orange and white, we waited for the church van. We had never been to an NFL game and couldn't have been more excited. We were hyped with enthusiasm as we speculated on how the game would turn out and who was gonna make the big play.

But the big play that day wasn't on the field—it was on us.

The church van never showed up.

I remember standing there, staring at the empty street, feeling the cold seep into my chest. "Are we still going?" I asked, as if somehow saying it out loud would fix things. But the answer never came.

That afternoon, I sat in my room listening to the game on the radio. Every cheer from the crowd felt like a punch to the gut. I had worked so hard, and it felt like none of it mattered.

I took it personally.

The next day, I made a decision. If I wanted to go to a game, I would have to make it happen myself. I grabbed my church fundraiser materials and hit the streets again.

I was almost there—just five dollars short—when it happened.

"Where are your credentials, young man?" the older lady asked while squinting at me over her glasses. "Where's something from your church saying what this is for?"

My face turned red. I didn't have anything. But I didn't have anything before, and no one had asked me for it.

"I'm calling your parents," she said, reaching for the phone. "I'll find out what this is all about."

Panic set in.

But I didn't run. She knew who I was and where I lived. This wasn't good. I just knew that as soon as my parents found out, I would be in trouble. BIG trouble.

When she hung up the phone, I hung up my dreams. I heard them tell her to send me straight home and that they'd take me to the church to make sure the money got to where I said it was going.

It was awful. Not only did I raise money once for the church with nothing in return, but now I've done it twice!

Ugh.

As an eleven-year-old kid in desperate need of funds, I was stuck. The options for work were limited. Garage sales were an option, but I didn't have much to sell. I could sell my baseball cards, but who would buy them?

So I did what any respectable kid in the 80s would do—I asked to use my dad's lawnmower.

Now, armed with something I could make money with, off I went.

"I'm raising money to go to a Buccaneers game," I told neighbors as I went door-to-door. "Can I cut your yard?"

It worked. I knocked and knocked and then cut and cut. Each yard, a new opportunity. More money, more responsibility. Many then wanted me to come back and cut it the following week.

All of a sudden, I had ten yards that I was doing in my neighborhood. Not just cutting but weed whipping, edging, and clean up. It was a great gig, but it was taking all my time.

Before long, I had made enough to go to a Buccaneers game with my dad. The Bucs lost that day, but the experience wasn't lost on me. The crowds, energy, and excitement were nothing like I'd ever seen.

I smiled for days and showed everybody at school the souvenir cup I had gotten at the game—the game I paid for myself.

Eight months later and still cutting, I discovered the power of delegation. My friend down the street needed money, and I needed help.

"You can use all my equipment," I offered, "and I'll handle the customers and clean up."

For the next two years we worked together and split the money. I'd supply the equipment, talk to the homeowners, and fix any problems while he'd do the work.

My plan worked beautifully. I learned to communicate customer expectations and resolve issues while he handled the labor. It was my first taste of leadership—and it was exhilarating.

Eventually, we both moved into other jobs, but the lessons stuck. That little lawn business taught me more about responsibility, entrepreneurship, and teamwork than any game ever could have.

But none of this story happened without that fundraiser and the subsequent disappointment that led me to a new way of thinking.

That moment was one of the best things that ever happened to me. It forced me to look inward and discover that I had the power to change my own life.

Instead of blaming others, I turned disappointment into drive. Instead of raising money, I built a business. Instead of complaining, I solved problems.

Dead ends are only the end if you stop. If you turn around and go in a different direction, there's no telling where you'll end up. And you just might find that the one thing you were looking for isn't the gold mine you end up finding in the end.

For me, the gold mine wasn't just the money I earned or the game I finally attended—it was the lessons that came with it.

Learning to turn frustration into fuel, to build something from scratch, and to empower others along the way wasn't part of the plan. But sometimes, life's greatest lessons come from its biggest letdowns.

That missed game taught me something no whistle or touchdown ever could—that I had the power to change my own life. I didn't have to wait for someone else to show up or for circumstances to align perfectly. I just had to take the first step.

Life will always have speed bumps, but they're only obstacles if you let them be. With the right perspective, they can become stepping stones to something far greater than you ever imagined.

And all it takes is a single moment to change your direction—and maybe, just maybe, your life.

MAKING IT MATTER

Essence of the Moment

Disappointment is only the end if you let it be. Turning obstacles into opportunities can uncover strengths, build resilience, and lead you to unexpected success.

Timeless Truths

- ☑ **Failure Fuels Growth:** The lessons from setbacks often teach us more than immediate success ever could.
- ☑ **Responsibility Drives Change:** Taking ownership of your challenges can open doors to personal transformation.
- ☑ **Opportunity is Everywhere:** Even the smallest ventures can lead to profound insights and lasting rewards.

1. **Reframe Setbacks:** Think back on a challenge you've faced recently. Today, take a moment to ask yourself what lesson or opportunity might be hiding within it.
2. **Take a Small Step:** Tackle a project or goal you've been hesitant to start—and do so this week. Focus on doing just one thing to move it forward.
3. **Empower Someone Else:** By the end of the month, share a skill, insight, or experience you've gained from overcoming obstacles. You might just inspire someone to take their own first step.

Next Level Thinking

Ask yourself:
- How do I typically respond to setbacks, and what can I do to handle them more constructively?
- What skills or strengths have I gained from past disappointments or challenges?
- Who in my life could benefit from my support, mentorship, or shared experiences?
- How can I take more ownership of the outcomes I want to achieve?

Insight to Remember

"Learning to turn frustration into fuel, to build something from scratch, and to empower others along the way wasn't part of the plan. But sometimes, life's greatest lessons come from its biggest letdowns."

26

HER BIGGEST FAN

Laying in the hospital, unable to move, I watched McKenzie cling to Joanna's leg. Breanna was hiding behind her.

She was terrified. She was in tears and didn't know what to do or say. All she knew was that her dad was lying there and might not get back up.

The doctors were not very optimistic. They said I had come down with a muscle-eating virus, and it was destroying my insides. There wasn't much they could do other than wait and see.

I desperately wanted McKenzie and Breanna to come to my side, but they wouldn't.

That's when I heard the words that would save my life. The words I would replay probably a thousand times over the next several days. The words that pushed me through when I had no strength to do anything else.

"Does this mean I'll never get to play with Daddy again?" she said while looking up at Joanna with a heartbroken face.

Talk about a gut punch. Yep—one of the most impactful moments of my life right there. Words that I kept replaying over and over.

When I got out of the hospital, my life changed. My priorities changed. My work balance changed. My desire to chase money changed. My involvement in my kids' lives changed.

From that moment forward, I was there. For just about everything.

I'd come to visit her at her preschool. I'd play with her and her class. We'd go to playgrounds. We'd walk at the malls. We'd drive and talk and play and do everything together.

Our family grew, and McKenzie became my little helper. My pal. My fishing partner. My cleaning partner. My chess partner. My singing partner (neither of us were great). My little sports partner. My little reading partner.

As the eldest of four, McKenzie got to do it all first. She'd try things and do them before her siblings. She loved being the one who was old enough and then always wanted her siblings to be able to join her.

She always wanted to learn and loved being a part of anything active. Baseball, football, golf, ice skating, dance, frisbee, gymnastics, and volleyball. She worked hard and developed an incredible work ethic, not just for sports, but everything she did.

She'd practice on her own and ask questions constantly. She used her time wisely and continuously wanted my feedback. She developed a love for art and was so creative. Painting, drawing, creating... all of it.

We talked every single day until just a couple of years ago. For most of her childhood, I'd spend upwards of an hour a night helping the four of them understand things in the world, and they made connections with everything. McKenzie was the leader of the pack and "got it" like no other.

Through middle school, McKenzie and I spoke frequently, but it was different. She was learning but spreading her wings. She was curious about the world and wanted to figure things out on her own. This didn't always work out at the moment, but, in a way, it did.

Trials and tribulations, friendships and relationships, sports, and her own business would define her high school period, where she buckled down and became her own person. Our talks became less frequent but more impactful. Our time together was less but valued more.

McKenzie has taken the brunt of all the mistakes our kids have made and has come out of it like a champ. Her leadership abilities have been strengthened. Her social skills have improved dramatically. Her work ethic has been tightened up. Her dedication to learning has been solidified.

Most impressively, McKenzie's ability to empathize and understand what others are going through is second to none. She's been hurt by friends. She's hurt others and taken ownership. She's had her hard work ruined by others. She's had her money stolen. She's endured poor leadership and dealt with angry customers.

And, I'm SO glad it all happened to her.

Because she bent but didn't break. She learned to accept disappointments and keep going. She learned to recognize the difference between subjective and objective awards. She learned to depend on herself.

Not long ago, she asked me to take her to school for the last time. It had been a while, but she wanted it to be like old times. Some of our best times and most meaningful talks were during our rides to and from school. That day was no different. When we arrived, I got out and hugged her and told her how proud I was. When she got home that afternoon, I hugged her again and said, "Congratulations!"

Later that night, she graduated high school and turned the page to start her next chapter. She wasn't ready, but then, who is? She graduated first in her class with a near 4.75GPA and would soon play golf in college. She was the recipient of a number of extremely meaningful scholarships and had the support of so many wonderful folks.

That day marked the end of an incredible chapter of her life, and mine.

I'm so incredibly proud of the young lady McKenzie has become, and will always be her biggest fan. I'm proud of what she's accomplished, but more proud of the person she is inside. She's the hardest working, easiest going, most thoughtful, dedicated, compassionate, smartest, and beautiful young lady out there.

Oh, and don't get me wrong. She has a wild side a mile wide and a tough side that'll rival the most hardened out there. She's trusting, but she's a thinker like no other. It's all part of the badge, and she wears it with honor. I believe in her, trust her judgment, and look forward to watching her continue to make a beautiful life out of what she was given.

I'm thankful to McKenzie for inspiring me and being my best friend for so long. For always believing in me and being the supporter she's been. For being a role model for her siblings and giving them something great to strive for. And for showing them a few mistakes along the way.

I couldn't have made it without her, and neither could they.

Being her dad has been my favorite eighteen-year stretch, and I'll cherish it forever.

And, as I sit here writing this with tears in my eyes, I can't help but ask the question,

"Does this mean I'll never get to play with McKenzie again?"

MAKING IT MATTER

Essence of the Moment

Parenthood is a journey filled with growth, resilience, and endless love. As we guide our children, they teach us invaluable lessons about perseverance, compassion, and the profound impact of shared moments.

Timeless Truths

☑ **Growth Through Challenges:** Resilience is born in facing and overcoming inevitable setbacks.

☑ **Moments Matter Most:** The seemingly small, everyday connections create the foundation of a lifelong bond.

☑ **Leadership by Example:** Guiding others is most impactful when accompanied by authenticity, vulnerability, and trust.

Bringing It Home

1. **Recognize the Little Wins:** Today, take a moment to acknowledge a small victory in someone's life—whether it's a family member, friend, or colleague.
2. **Be Fully Present:** Dedicate some uninterrupted time this week to connect with someone you care about. A simple car ride, a dinner together, or a shared activity can create memories that last a lifetime.
3. **Celebrate Growth:** Take the time this month to write a letter or have a heartfelt conversation with someone you've watched grow. Share your pride in their journey and encourage them for what's next.

Next Level Thinking

Ask yourself:
- How can I create more opportunities for meaningful moments with those I love?
- What lessons have my challenges taught me that I can share with others?
- How can I show my belief in someone else's potential to help them thrive?
- What can I do to model resilience and compassion in my own life?

Insight to Remember

"Because, she bent, but didn't break. She learned to accept disappointments and keep going. She learned to recognize the difference between subjective and objective awards. She learned to depend on herself."

27

BEYOND THE SURGE

When I first picked up the phone I thought it was just another check-in. You know, "Hey bud, how's it going?" Or, it could have been like the last time when it was a two-hour talk about building a business.

Nope. This time was different. This time, it got real—fast. Like, the kind of real and fast that puts people into action. And changes lives.

The moment I hung up the phone, I told Joanna the story. That we needed to help. And that we'd have to pull our son out of high school to do it.

An hour later, we'd talked through everything and decided it was a go. Except, we hadn't told my son yet.

When we told him he lit right up. "So, we get to go to Florida and help people dig out and rebuild their lives?"

Yep.

We were in a rental car three days later and on our way to Ft. Myers Beach. Two weeks prior, they had been devastated by a massive storm surge and pummeled by the winds of Hurricane Ian. Our friends were there in the middle of it, and they needed help, fast!

We arrived at our campsite at nearly eleven at night, unloaded, and were told to be ready by five to start heading towards the beach. We were exhausted from a long day, but excited to be with people who were pumped about helping others.

Having lived in Florida for over thirty years, I had seen wind damage and some destruction, but nothing prepared me for what I was about to see.

From ten miles out, there were trees down regularly. A few windows boarded here and there, and a few signs looked like they were experiencing a hangover from the night before.

Five miles out, the number of trees down is ten-fold what it was. The trees that remain have been stripped of any greenery whatsoever. It's eerie. Debris is starting to be seen and line the streets. It's not awful yet, but it's getting worse.

Three miles out, it's starting to look like a war zone. We see cars that are flipped. Boats on their side. Power lines are down. Random pieces of buildings just sitting in parking lots. And the debris on the side of the road is easily six feet high and probably ten feet wide in spots.

Two miles from the beach, I'm in absolute shock. I'm astonished at what I'm seeing. There are literal yachts on the highway easily fifty to sixty feet long. And about a hundred other boats all stacked up on the side and into the wooded area. But there isn't water here. At all. Boats are in trees, for crying out loud.

We make it through the police barricade they'd set up to keep onlookers out and go over the main bridge to the beach. "Oh my God" I hear, over and over. As far as we could see, boats were stacked up and crushed on top of one another, probably by the thousands. Massive fishing vessels and shrimp boats were right in the mix.

Witnessing the storm's aftermath firsthand was a moment I'll never forget. As we made it onto the beach, my heart sank.

Large hotels that were booming just weeks earlier—shut down. Smaller hotels that lined the beach on both sides—gone. Many were completely erased from their foundations. Stores were the same way. You could see where buildings had been but were no longer. Anything that was still there was unrecognizable. It was reminiscent of a ghost town but on the beach.

When we got into the neighborhoods, it became even more surreal. Roads were gone. Signage was gone. Sand was everywhere. Many houses had just disappeared. Waterlines were visible on every structure—many were well over ten feet high.

And, get this—there were people from the neighborhoods just walking around and helping others everywhere they could. It was breathtaking.

Over the next six weeks, we'd find ourselves amid some of the worst destruction you could imagine, with the most beautiful souls who had a new perspective on what "life's storms" meant.

People who once valued "things" were now grateful and happy to be alive. They'd seen the worst of the storm, buried their friends and neighbors, and now did their best to piece together any semblance of normalcy they could.

Day after day, we heard stories of heartbreak, loss, and survival. And how it turned into compassion, hope, and love. Many people had lived there their entire lives, and they were now left with nothing but a shell of a house and memories.

Or nothing at all.

The small team we were a part of was remarkable and gave people hope. Besides me and my son, the core team comprised four key characters: Jeremy, Troy, Yadon, and Andreas. They were talented, hard-working, and thorough—all traits that helped them knock out a ton of work and help countless families.

Best of all, that team took my son under their wing and gave him the experience of a lifetime. They were mentors at a time when he needed it most. They had high expectations of him, gave him chances, and held him accountable.

We put in well over five hundred hours in the mud, mold, and mystery grime, but it was worth every moment. Except for the cold showers—if I never take another one again, it'll be too soon.

That six-week stint taught me and my son more than any book could have. About people. About resilience. About loss. About rebuilding. About showing up and making things happen. About communities. About connection. And about the power of the human spirit.

Those that were left standing were changed people. I'm proud to have met them and to have helped them rebuild in the time that we were there.

Moments like this are rare, but they matter—to everyone involved. To all my friends in Ft. Myers now, thank you for letting us be a part of your lives and for accepting us as neighbors.

Because we're all neighbors in this worldwide community we live in.

MAKING IT MATTER

Essence of the Moment

Resilience shines brightest in the darkest times. When communities unite, human connection and compassion rebuild what storms have taken away.

Timeless Truths

☑ **Challenges Forge Strength:** The hardest trials often reveal the depth of our resilience and humanity.

☑ **Community Creates Hope:** True recovery comes not just from rebuilding homes but from rebuilding lives together.

☑ **Mentorship Multiplies Impact:** Teaching others through action and accountability leaves a lasting legacy.

Bringing It Home

1. **Lend a Helping Hand:** Take some time today to identify someone around you who could use extra support. Even a small gesture can make a difference.

2. **Build Bridges:** This week, reach out to a community group, neighborhood effort, or local cause where you can lend your skills or time to help others.
3. **Reflect and Connect:** Before the end of the month, organize a meaningful conversation or gathering with friends or family to reflect on shared challenges and celebrate the connections that saw you through them.

Next Level Thinking

Ask yourself:
- How can I better respond to challenges with resilience and purpose?
- Who in my life could benefit from my support or mentorship, and how can I help them thrive?
- What lessons have I learned from difficult times that I can share with others to inspire hope?
- How can I contribute to building stronger connections in my community or network?

Insight to Remember

"People who once valued "things" were now just full of gratitude and happy to be alive."

28

THE POWER OF SIX

Six words.

I've had so many conversations—explanations of this, that, and the other.

Way more than six words on my side... probably more like six thousand. All to people I know who have been there and done that.

It's a lot of moving parts. Kids. Business. House. Trips. Cars. Memberships. Credit cards. Groceries. Repairs. Clothing. Birthday parties. Award ceremonies. Everyday bills.

You know, the regular stuff.

But then there's inflation, gas, variable interest rates, hospital bills, and broken-down vehicles.

Yep, sometimes we get hit by a right hook, and then it's followed by an uppercut. We stand, but we're wobbly. We're on the verge of going down, but we're staggering.

The knockout punch could come at any moment.

Then, out of nowhere, comes those six words. Completely unexpected, but needed. Like when a plane with no landing gear glides smoothly onto a landing strip.

No judgment. No guilt trips. No laughing. No kicking someone while they're down. Just another human doing what humans do best. Being human.

"What can I do to help?" Shawn said in his rough, Italian voice that blends well with a Philly accent.

That's it. Just those six words. They shut me down. They stopped me cold. They caused a much-needed pause.

A pin dropped, and I heard it.

It went from someone listening to putting me on the spot. The moment of truth. The nuts and bolts that were scattered all along the floor near me needed to be put together.

"What can I do to help?" I hear again.

I swallowed hard. My mind was racing. I knew the silence was awkward, but it was real.

Short term, the answer is money. Long term, the answer is exposure. It's a vicious cycle. You need money to make money, but exposure in the form of visibility is so incredibly valuable as the long tail is where it's at. But money helps in the short run.

Thoughts ran through my head, but I couldn't verbalize them yet. I was the proverbial fish—on the hook.

So I answered from a place of complete humility. Shawn's response, though, put me at ease. He made me feel as though we were in the same boat and he was my co-captain—that my problem was his problem because that's what we do for one another.

We kept talking. He kept asking questions. I explained and shared what I could about all that was going on.

He got it. Then he took action.

It was that easy.

He could tell it had been weighing on me. That I'd not had the chance to talk about, promote or market any of our products and that it was needed.

He wasn't the first person I talked to about it. Nor the second. Nor the tenth.

But he *was* the first to use those six words—and nothing but.

And it meant something to me. It hit much harder than I expected. It was a moment of deep connection on a level I've not felt in years.

It was so simple, yet effective. And it has universal appeal. It's a phrase we can all use instead of "What do you need?" or "Man, that sucks!" or "I hope you get it figured out," or "Well, good luck with that."

Look where the focus is. "What can I" as in: me, the person saying it… What can I personally be a part of and take ownership of? "Do" as in: an action word, to take some sort of action on my own without you. "To help" as in: to make a difference to YOU.

The focus here is ALL on the person using the phrase. So different.

Those six words, to me, said we're in it together. That we're a team, and I'm not alone. That someone else out there is willing to help me with something that has nothing to do with them.

And that's why, today, I'm locking it in. I'm making sure those six words—as an open-ended question—become a staple for me to ask of others. I want to be the one asking the question. I want to be the one waiting for someone to figure it out.

Perhaps you'll want to try it, too? If you discover that you have a friend in need, find a way to ask, "What can I do to help?"

If you say it and mean it, it can have a tremendous effect on the receiver.

MAKING IT MATTER

Essence of the Moment

Sometimes, the most straightforward question holds the most profound power. Asking "What can I do to help?" can turn someone's struggle into shared strength and build bonds that truly matter.

Timeless Truths

- ☑ **Words Carry Weight:** A single sentence, spoken sincerely, can make an immeasurable difference.
- ☑ **Help Begins with Action:** True support comes not from intentions, but the actions you're willing to take.

☑ **Connection Heals:** Offering help isn't just about solving problems—it's about reminding others they're not alone.

Bringing It Home

1. **Reach Out Sincerely:** Think of a friend or family member who might be facing challenges. A simple, heartfelt "What can I do to help?" could start a powerful conversation today.
2. **Follow Through:** If someone shares how you can assist them this week, don't just nod along—take tangible action to lighten their load and show that your offer wasn't just words.
3. **Make It a Habit:** Keep track of the number of times you've asked this question throughout the month and take note of the responses. Look for ways to make it a natural part of your interactions moving forward.

Next Level Thinking

Ask yourself:

▷ How often do I offer help with sincerity and intention?
▷ In what ways can I take ownership of the support I offer to others?
▷ Who in my life might benefit from being asked this question right now?
▷ How can I inspire others to adopt this personal support mindset?

Insight to Remember

> *"Those six words, to me, said we're in it together. That we're a team and I'm not alone. That someone else out there is willing to help me with something that has nothing to do with them."*

29

FERTILIZER

The guy I was there to see was busy. His name was Terry. The lady at the front desk said he was wrapping something up and would be available shortly.

This was in a fertilizer company where there wasn't exactly a waiting area, so I just stood in front of her... and waited.

Seconds after the silence started, she received a message on her phone. Seconds after that, I heard her grumbling about something that sounded familiar.

She set her phone back down, and my smile lit up.

"Have you ever heard of a guy named Dr. David Martin?" I asked. It was related to her grumbling, and it started a conversation. A conversation that would go down as one of my favorites.

Shortly after I started the conversation, my friend showed up, talked with me briefly, then had to get back to work. But I stayed. Though I came for fertilizer that day and to speak with my friend, I left with a whole new appreciation for someone great at conversing.

Her name is Tammy.

What I saw that morning wasn't a receptionist but a sophisticated woman who was merely filling a job. She was an active listener in every sense of the word. Facial expressions, repeating key concepts, writing things down, asking questions, looking things up, and adding to the conversation—yep, it was all that and then some.

Before I knew it, we'd been talking for an hour. And we'd just begun. Two hours in, and the momentum was fierce. Three hours, and it felt like it had only been a minute. Four hours in, and we were just getting somewhere.

And then, my phone rang.

"Where's the fertilizer?" I hear from Joanna, who's out in the yard and wondering what had happened.

That would end our talk, but not our friendship.

Over the next couple of years, Tammy and I would message back and forth about life, our children, the state of the world, and what kinds of things we both found interesting. Long messages, too. Thoughtful ones where we'd give our analysis and what our takeaways were. And we'd talk online regularly.

Then, one day, I was talking with a mutual friend in a store when I saw a beautiful car pull up and park. I commented on it, and my friend said, you know that's Tammy's husband, right? So cool! And no, I didn't know him. Yet.

Moments later, we were shaking hands and talking like old friends. Because, in a way, we were. We had both heard about each other but had never met.

That sparked even more conversations with Tammy and further strengthened our friendship.

We get to choose when to speak up and start a conversation, but we don't get to choose how they react. When we speak up and find that someone else reacts in a way that truly impresses us, we have to be willing to make something of the moment.

I'm so glad to have spoken up that day. Tammy has brought so much into my life in the way of enlightenment, friendship, generosity, and authenticity, and it's helped me bridge gaps with others.

And this is why it's important to not judge others for their jobs. Tammy has gone on to do other wonderful things in her life, and she continues to impress me with her wisdom, insight, and kindness.

So, friends, the next time you have downtime, engage someone in conversation. You have no idea what you're embarking upon, and you just might get lucky and find your own Tammy to brag about.

Because, after all, friendships can bloom with a bit of fertilizer in the form of love and nurturing.

MAKING IT MATTER

Essence of the Moment

Friendships often start in the most unexpected places. When we take the time to engage genuinely, we open the door to connections that can enrich our lives and transform the ordinary into something extraordinary.

Timeless Truths

- ☑ **Conversations Create Bridges:** A single thoughtful conversation can lead to meaningful relationships that last a lifetime.
- ☑ **General Interest Inspires:** Truly listening and engaging with someone can uncover wisdom and connection in surprising places.
- ☑ **Friendships Need Nurturing:** Like plants, relationships grow best when we care for them with authenticity and effort.

Bringing It Home

1. **Start a Conversation:** Maybe today's the day you strike up a conversation with someone you wouldn't normally engage with. It doesn't have to be profound—just a kind word or a curious question could be enough to spark something meaningful.
2. **Revisit an Old Connection:** Sometime this week, reach out to someone who's been on your mind. Maybe it's an old friend or

someone you've admired but haven't talked to in a while. A quick text or call could be the start of something deeper.

3. **Nurture a Friendship:** By the end of the month, think about someone who's shown they value your time and make an effort to invest in that connection. Grab coffee, send them a thoughtful note, or just spend a little extra time with them. You might be surprised at what blooms.

Next Level Thinking

Ask yourself:
- How often do I truly listen when someone speaks, and how could I improve?
- What opportunities have I missed to connect with someone because I was too focused on my own agenda?
- Who in my life deserves more of my time and attention, and how can I prioritize them?
- What unexpected friendships or lessons could I find by engaging with someone I might typically overlook?

Insight to Remember

"Because, after all, friendships can bloom with a bit of fertilizer in the form of love and nurturing."

30

IMPRESSIONS

Every now and then we see someone and just know we won't like them. We don't know the first thing about them, but something tells us we won't connect. And we're just sure of it.

Well, from a distance, as I was walking up, I saw the guy running the show. I thought he'd be grumpy, stuffy, reserved, and hard to work with. Within seconds of meeting him, shaking his hand firmly, and watching his genuine smile form, my impression changed.

I was wrong. All my preconceived notions—wrong. My first impression—wrong. All wrong in a single moment.

I happen to be someone who, if I like how you do business and treat people, will come back again and again and will tell people about you repeatedly.

Well, friends, his name is Bill. Bill Moore, to be specific. My kids and I know him as Mr. Bill.

Mr. Bill runs the Southeast Kentucky Junior Golf Tour and has done so for over twenty-five years now. And for the last six years, I've had the pleasure of working with him one-on-one, and I've been nothing but impressed.

Here's what I've learned.

Mr. Bill cares. He cares about people, and it shows. He's not the most sophisticated nor the most technical, but he might vie for the title of the one who cares about people the most. Plus, he's got an incredible aura about him—an infectious energy. He goes out of his way to appease both adults and kids alike.

Week after week, tournament after tournament, he plans, preps, sets up, buys trophies for, works with courses, coordinates with parents, talks to players, shows up early, converses with everyone, brings drinks and snacks, tallies scores, gives awards, takes pictures, and creates meaningful posts for the kids.

And, at the end of each year, he does his own awards ceremony where he talks about the players, the highlights from the year, hand-makes his own special trophies complete with pictures of the players, and congratulates the players individually.

He doesn't do it for the money—he does it because he wants to create an experience. And an experience is precisely what he's created. It's not like the big tournaments, but it's one where all four of my kids have said, yearly, that they want to play in HIS tournaments because it's more about playing the game and enjoying the camaraderie than just "winning."

In other words, it's the way golf should be played.

Do they have rules officials? No. He does that, too. Well, it's him and his assistant, Tanner, who's just as pleasant and likable as Mr. Bill. Do they have live scoring? Yes. Meaning, you write your score down on your card as you go... live. Past that, no, it's not live. Does he have fancy signs, billboards, banners, or even his own custom tee box markers with his branding? Also, no.

What he does have, however, is far more important. A love for the game and a love for the kids. He just goes out there and makes it work without all the fancy-shmancy gadgets that are available. He wants the kids to enjoy themselves and get their feet wet with competition.

Truth be told, I've watched Mr. Bill interact with young golfers, their parents, and their grandparents for years and have truly been impressed time and time again. He uses expressions like, "Whatever works for you guys," "Do what's best for your family," "Don't worry about it," and "Just pay me next time" regularly. More times than I can count, I've seen people leave conversations with him smiling and thankful for how he's handled situations.

Does he get frustrated? Absolutely. I've heard about his struggles and the situations he deals with, but he's always ended with a can-do attitude and the goal of making things right for the kids.

Never once have I seen him take advantage of someone or make things difficult for a player or a parent the way other tour directors have, and I've complimented him for it. He handles difficulties with poise and grace, and I've applauded him many times.

I've even spoken with those who run the courses he uses, and they've ALL been super complimentary of him and love what he does for the kids. I've not heard the first complaint about him or his tour, and that matters because of how many people are involved and how many lives it touches.

So, I'd like to celebrate. Not a birthday or an anniversary or anything like that, just a person doing the best he can to add something to the world in the best way he knows how. Today, I will celebrate those who have the kids' best interest at heart when it comes to golf and doing the right thing—and the one person I can think of is Bill Moore. And for the record, I've worked with and dealt with a LOT of event directors.

I raise my glass to you, Mr. Bill, and say, "Thanks for a wonderful run! I wish you continued successes over the years and hope everyone gets a chance to meet you in person and experience such wonderful customer service."

Friends, if you know of anyone looking to compete in golf and they're anywhere near south-central or southeast Kentucky, please share my recommendation with them and try his tour for yourself.

And I'll close this story with this.

Sometimes we're wrong about people. We judge before we know anything. We decide who they are in our minds before we give them a chance to make their actual impression. And when we do that, we miss out on everything that person has built in their life. We lose the opportunity to see the person for who they really are.

Today, I'm thankful for moments like this. When I'm pleasantly surprised to see the world from a different perspective just by meeting someone new.

MAKING IT MATTER

Sometimes, first impressions lead us astray. By taking the time to truly see people for who they are, we open ourselves to deeper connections and unexpected inspiration.

Timeless Truths

☑ **Judgment Blocks Opportunity:** Snap judgments can rob us of meaningful relationships.

☑ **Passion Creates Impact:** Genuine care and dedication leave lasting impressions.

☑ **Kindness Builds Legacy:** A consistent commitment to treating people well builds a reputation that resonates far beyond immediate interactions.

Bringing It Home

1. **Pause Before Judging:** Today, when you meet someone new or revisit an existing connection, take a moment to check your assumptions. Instead of making a snap judgment, let their actions guide your perspective.
2. **Look for the Passion:** Over the next couple of weeks, take note of the people who truly care about what they're doing, whether at work, in your community, or even within your family. Acknowledge their efforts—it might mean more than you think.
3. **Celebrate Someone's Impact:** By the end of the month, reach out to someone whose work or attitude has positively affected you. Share your gratitude, whether it's through a quick note, a phone call, or even a public shout-out. Let them know the difference they've made.

Next Level Thinking

Ask yourself:
- What assumptions have I made recently that might need re-evaluating?
- Who in my life consistently goes above and beyond, and how can I show my appreciation?
- How does my own passion for what I do influence those around me?
- In what ways can I create opportunities for others to leave a better impression of themselves?

Insight to Remember

"Sometimes we're wrong about people. We judge before we know anything. We decide who they are in our minds before we give them a chance to make their actual impression."

31

LIFE'S RHYTHMS

The whistles blew, and everything stopped.

Coaches sprinted toward the field, their faces tense with concern. My teammates stood frozen and wide-eyed as they watched me struggle while spitting up blood.

As a wide receiver, there's an inherent risk in going across the middle. But passion blinds you to fear, and make no mistake—football was my passion.

Until it wasn't.

The hit was brutal and left me gasping for air, clutching my throat. An upward-angled elbow that connected just under my helmet. The pain was sharp, but the fear was sharper.

"Your larynx was severely damaged," the doctor explained. "If you take another hit, you'll likely lose your voice permanently."

I was given the choice to keep playing and risk losing it all or hanging up my cleats. The choice should have been easy, but it wasn't. Football wasn't just a sport to me—it was my identity. Past that, it was a lifelong passion and my ticket to college.

For a solid two weeks, I held onto hope, even as my voice faded and my throat ached with every breath. At my follow-up appointment, the doctor didn't mince words.

"No more contact sports for you. Period."

I've been hit hard, but nothing hit as hard as that moment. It was a tough one to swallow—literally. My dreams, or whatever was left of them, dissolved in an instant.

I felt like I had been robbed—my identity, hopes, and dreams —all of it, gone. Stripped clean and just left beaten and bruised on the side of the road.

The following weeks felt like a blur. I had more free time than ever, but ironically, it came at a price. Mentally, I was taking a beating. I was stuck in a loop, replaying the injury in my head and getting angrier with every thought.

"Why did this happen to me?"

I spent a lot of time driving, listening to music, and feeling sorry for myself. A lot of thinking occurs on long drives, especially when you're supposed to be in school. Well, it wasn't long before I received my first speeding ticket, and things started spiraling downward.

"You can't just keep moping around and not doing anything," my mom said one afternoon. "You need something else to focus on."

"I'm not moping," I muttered. "I'm just driving around."

"Well, since you got a speeding ticket, you're grounded. And you're coming with me tonight."

"Where?"

"You'll see. We have to be there at 5, so get yourself looking decent by 4:30."

"Do I really have to go?" I groaned, utterly uninterested in what I thought was some pointless punishment for my inability to follow traffic laws.

Yeah, well, you've heard the statement, *you don't know what you don't know*... it's true.

An entirely different world would present itself to me at 5 o'clock. By 5:15, I was standing in a dimly lit, mirrored ballroom studio, arms crossed, feeling like a fish out of water.

The studio smelled like a combination of wood polish, Old Spice, and old lady perfume. People three to five times my age milled about, chatting and laughing. Meanwhile, I was plotting my escape.

Then, she walked in.

Jeannie. A 24-year-old dance instructor with the kind of poise and presence that made the whole room stop. Her smile was warm, her voice inviting, and her every movement seemed to increase my body temperature by a degree or two.

"Hi, I'm Jeannie," she said, extending her hand. "Let's get started!"

I felt like time had stopped right then and there. I'd never intentionally touched an older woman, and certainly not one that looked like her. Her hand, suspended in the air, looked like it had a glowing light in my mind's eye—and a magnet that slowly drew my hand to her without me thinking.

Before I knew it, I was over in the corner with her, trying to figure out how to walk, move, and breathe—all at once.

"Put your right hand here," she said. Don't have to ask me twice! "Now step like this. Good! And don't forget to breathe."

Ha. Breathe? Nope. I wasn't breathing. Or thinking. Or functioning normally, really. Her minty breath, body spray, and hair scent were completely intoxicating. And disarming.

"It's okay," she reassured me every time I fumbled. "You're doing great!" Was I though?

When the lesson ended, my mom asked, "How was it?"

"Terrible!" I replied. "When's my next one?"

Three days later, I showed up again. But this time, it was different. I had spent some seventy-one hours thinking about it and preparing. Gum? Check. Deodorant? Check. Freshly trimmed nails? Check. Cleanly shaven? Check. A splash of cologne? Double check.

Jeannie greeted me with a hug, and just like that, all my doubts and fears disappeared, and I started to breathe again.

Over the next six weeks, I'd see Jeannie at least twenty different times. Rhythm I didn't know I had was forming, and dances I didn't know existed were what I was practicing.

Who knew my background in athletics would play such a prominent role in my new pastime? Remember those doctor orders regarding contact sports—yeah, well, he was wrong. I'd discovered the best contact sport of all—and it was co-ed. Score!

Then, one day, I heard a radio ad promoting "Teen Nights" at a country nightclub in Tampa. Ages 13 to 18, and dancing lessons started at 7.

"You should go," Jeannie encouraged. Then she helped me

understand how to convert dances from ballroom to country—and just like that, a whole new window of opportunity was unlocked.

That first night, I showed up early, only to stand in line behind hundreds of other teens. Nerves battled with excitement as we all made our way to the swinging doors. When I walked in, it was like I had entered an old Western saloon, and my paradigm shifted once again.

The music was loud, the energy electric, and the club was packed with teens dressed in their country best. And by best, I'm talking girls with new cowboy hats, boots, short skirts, and flashy tops.

At first, I stuck to just the line dancing—Electric slide, Boot Scootin' Boogie, and the newly released Achy Breaky Heart—they were all the rage. Then, they did a mixer called Wild Wild West, where the guys would dance with every girl on the floor—I was hooked.

About ten seconds—that's how long you'd dance with each girl. Just enough time for me to introduce myself, ask for the girl's name, say something specific about their outfit or hair or boots, and then thank them for the dance.

This was the perfect way for me to practice manners and conversation skills and—you guessed it—meet girls. It was a game-changer for a 16-year-old. Before long, I'd met every girl who knew how to dance, and soon, my dance card was filled with girls who wanted to dance the swing, two-step, and the occasional waltz.

"You're really good at this," a girl named Michelle said as we danced. "You're so easy to dance with!"

That one compliment was all it took. I was no longer just a guy who had lost football—I was a guy who found a way to connect with girls in a way that mattered.

Night after night, I'd show up early and close the place down. Word spread fast at school.

"Why do all the girls want to dance with you?" my football friends asked.

"Because I know how," I replied with a grin.

Before long, I was teaching them—and I LOVED it! On nights when the club wasn't open, we cleared living rooms and broke out the CDs. I showed them what to do, how to lead, and how to make their partners feel special.

Surprisingly, etiquette isn't something we all just wake up with one day. Apparently, it has to be taught—and there has to be a reason for learning. Well, my friends and I had the best reason of all —girls.

We became a crew. A group of guys who traded cleats for boots and Friday night lights for the dance floors. Week after week, our group grew. More and more kids from our high school noticed and started joining in, and one night, we had well over a hundred from my school alone—which was some thirty miles from the club.

All this, from a dream that ended. An accident on the field that left me lost. Sometimes, dreams get cut short in order for us to wake up—and that's exactly what happened to me.

Jeannie's patience and encouragement sparked something in me on that first encounter. She helped me see that sometimes, the very thing you think is a setback is actually a road being paved for something much greater in your life.

Dance taught me about connection, confidence, and the importance of showing up for others. It opened my eyes to a world I didn't know existed, and learning to teach allowed me to explore human dynamics in a way that fueled excitement.

Life can change in an instant. We don't always understand the "why" in the moment, but when we look back, it shines like a beacon in the night. My first dance lesson wasn't just a step in the right direction—it was a step into a whole new way of life. One I'll forever be grateful for.

MAKING IT MATTER

Essence of the Moment

Life's detours often lead to destinations we never knew existed. Sometimes, what feels like a loss can become the beginning of something extraordinary.

Timeless Truths

- ☑ **Setbacks Spark Discovery:** What seems like an ending might just be the start of something new.
- ☑ **Patience Ignites Potential:** The encouragement of others can uncover talents we didn't know we had.
- ☑ **Passion Fuels Connection:** Finding what lights you up can help you connect with others in meaningful ways.

Bringing It Home

1. **Find Your Next Step:** Start today by reflecting on something you've lost or a dream that's been cut short. What's one new activity, hobby, or challenge you've always been curious about but haven't tried? Take the first step to explore it.
2. **Step Into the Unfamiliar:** This week, commit to stepping out of your comfort zone. Whether it's attending a new class, connecting with someone who inspires you, or revisiting an old passion in a new way, let the experience guide you toward discovery.
3. **Share the Journey:** By the end of the month, focus on how your newfound rhythm or activity can bring value to others. Whether it's sharing your progress, helping someone else learn, or simply inviting others to join, use your journey to inspire connection and growth.

Next Level Thinking

Ask yourself:
- How do I respond when a setback forces me to change direction?
- What passions have I overlooked or let go of that I could explore again?
- Am I willing to step outside my comfort zone to discover something new about myself?
- How can I use my own experiences to help someone else find their rhythm?

Insight to Remember

"Sometimes dreams get cut short in order for us to wake up—and that's exactly what happened to me."

32

HOW SWEET IT IS

Who knew a box of chocolates could teach such valuable lessons?

It was the fundraiser of all fundraisers—the one to get us to the Cub Scout Olympics.

This was a big deal in New Hampshire, where my Cub Scout Pack had been working hard on our projects as well as our physical fitness.

For weeks, we'd been tallying the sales—19 from Keith, 17 from Ammon, 15 from Scott, 14 from John, and mine was a mere 13. The struggle was real—for all of us—especially in a small town. We were all at wit's end. And our hopes of hitting our target started fading.

I had already hit up all my friends, the teachers at school, and the front office staff. Luckily, my favorite waitress at our town's one little restaurant had just bought a few for her kids—but we were a long way away.

"There has to be a better way," I sighed, slumping at the table, my face buried in my hands. "I've asked everyone I know, and I'm nowhere near eighty. None of us are—and we only have two weeks left!"

We were told that each of us had to sell eighty candy-bars. As eight-year-olds, this didn't seem hard—until it did. We didn't exactly have a lot going on in our lives other than school and Cub Scouts, so this really started to wear on us.

"And if we don't sell enough as a pack, we won't be able to go?" I asked with both concern and dread.

A few more days go by and we're up probably ten more bars as a pack—not good. I asked my mom if she could take me to the big grocery store in the next county over so I could stand outside and ask everyone who walked in.

"I just need people I can talk to!"

She agreed, and the next thing I knew, it was Saturday. Now armed with boxes and boxes of candy bars, I was ready to try something new—selling candy to strangers.

Was I dressed up in my schnazzy cub scout uniform? Oh yeah. Did I stand out with my bright red hair and big, confident smile? Undoubtedly. Did I hesitate to start conversations with every single person that walked in and out of the store? Not at all.

"You look like someone who loves a good chocolate bar," I'd say, waving one in front of them with a big grin. "It's only a dollar—and trust me, it's an instant mood booster!"

That was a fun one that got a lot of people laughing. Some people said they didn't like chocolate and tried to kill the conversation immediately.

"That's okay—I bet you know at least two kids that would do anything for one of these. And right now you can buy two for just two dollars!"

Winner. Over and over.

Some folks had large families—and somehow, I didn't let them get past me without everyone getting a chocolate bar in their hands.

Don't have change? "That's okay, you can pay for it on your way out—here, take the bar with you now and enjoy it!"

Boom, fifty sales in the first hour. And I was just getting started.

Every car that pulled into the parking lot that day was about to make a new friend—I just knew it. Everyone heard my story and how they'd be helping to get our pack to the Cub Scout Olympics. I even had to demonstrate my push-ups and sit-ups a few times just to make a sale—and it worked.

Well over a hundred sales in, and we're only two hours into the day. "There's a lady and her son walking up over there!" I'd hear and quickly mobilize so I could walk and talk with them. Again, new friends and new customers.

High-fives every time. From the customers and my parents, who were there watching.

Chalk it up to the fact that I really wanted everyone to be happy—and I honestly thought they'd be happy with a chocolate bar in their bellies. Because, why not? Chocolate made me happy, so it just made sense. Every time someone smiled and thanked me, my day got a little bit better.

Two hundred in, I'm yet to even take a break. I was well over a fifty percent conversion rate, and, if I'm being honest, I was bothered by the fact that it wasn't a hundred percent. Really bothered.

If we hadn't run out of candy bars, I might still be there. All three hundred and twelve chocolate bars we had found new homes that day.

I was told I set the sales record, but I'd later learn that records weren't really kept. Doesn't matter—I'll still own it just because.

I did, however, raise enough for our entire pack to make it to the Cub Scout Olympics that year and everyone was so relieved—but that wasn't the best part. For me, it was that I discovered how much I enjoyed connecting with people and helping them find something they didn't know they were looking for.

"I can't believe you sold all our chocolate bars! How'd you do it?" said everyone at our next meeting.

My answer revealed what I'd discovered. That it wasn't just selling a chocolate bar—it was a promise of an escape. A moment of joy wrapped in shiny paper. A way to spark a smile, start a conversation, and a little gift to make someone's day brighter.

You may be wondering about the Cub Scout Olympics and how it ended. Well, that was one where they really did keep track of things—and if you're ever curious, look it up, and you'll see a kid that looks a whole lot like me with a medal around his neck and the Governor of New Hampshire smiling right beside him. True story.

All because of the moment I went from selling candy bars to building relationships. When I went from trying to make money to trying to make people smile, laugh, and enjoy conversations. And to this day, that moment stands out as a significant life lesson.

A life lesson with a universal truth—find a way to improve someone else's day, and you're guaranteed to brighten your own. Get them laughing, and you'll reap the benefit. Get them smiling, and you can't help but do the same. Focus on others, and you'll always win in the end—even if you don't make it to the Olympics.

MAKING IT MATTER

Essence of the Moment

A simple goal, like selling candy bars, can transform into something much greater when you focus on connecting with people, spreading joy, and building relationships. True success comes from making others smile and finding shared moments of happiness.

Timeless Truths

- ☑ **Joy is Contagious:** A smile, a laugh, or a kind gesture can spark a ripple effect that brightens the day for everyone it touches.
- ☑ **Connection Transcends Transactions:** When you make people feel seen and valued, even the smallest interactions become meaningful.
- ☑ **Helping Others Fuels Success:** Focusing on how you can serve others creates outcomes far beyond what you set out to achieve.

Bringing It Home

1. **Think Beyond the Sale:** Next time you interact with someone, ask yourself how you can bring a little joy into the moment—

whether it's through a kind word, a smile, or even a small gesture.

2. **Focus on Relationships:** As you go through this week, look for ways to turn routine interactions into opportunities for connection. It might be a quick chat with a neighbor, extra effort in your customer service, or just finding common ground with someone you normally pass by.

3. **Celebrate Your Impact:** By the end of the month, reflect on the little moments where you've made someone smile or feel seen. Whether it's a compliment, encouragement, or shared laughter, celebrate the impact you've made and think about how to carry that forward.

Next Level Thinking

Ask yourself:

▷ When was the last time I focused entirely on someone else's happiness or success?

▷ How do I typically approach everyday interactions—with the goal of connection or completion?

▷ In what ways can I use my skills and talents to bring joy to others?

▷ What small act of kindness could I do today that might create a lasting memory for someone else?

Insight to Remember

"A life lesson with a universal truth—find a way to improve someone else's day, and you're guaranteed to brighten your own. Get them laughing, and you'll reap the benefit. Get them smiling, and you can't help but do the same. Focus on others, and you'll always win in the end—even if you don't make it to the Olympics."

33

OUTSTANDING

You've heard the term "outstanding in her field," right? When I first met this lady, that's exactly what she was doing. She was out, standing in her field.

Her field just happened to be a parking lot where she was hand-delivering a box of wine to a little old lady.

She was right next to my car door and I could hear the conversation clear as day—that little old lady was ready to par-tay! As for the delivery lady, I could feel the warmth from her smile. I could hear the authenticity in her voice. And I could see how much she truly cared by the way she treated this lady.

Moments later, she would find me inside and treat me the exact same way. A way that, to this day, reminds me of true Southern hospitality.

When she learned I was new to the area, she shifted into fifth gear and never let off. She opened up in a way you could only hope for and with wit and humor that kept me on my toes.

Moments later, she introduced me to her co-workers to ensure I had people to talk to if she wasn't there. Then, she introduced me to her favorite customers as they came in. She made it a point to use my name, tell them a little about me, and let them know I was new to town.

"Welcome to our home!" I'd hear, over and over. Before I knew it, I'd been in her store a little over two hours.

When I got home, I told Joanna all about Jo. How wonderful and welcoming she was. And that I thought they should meet.

A couple of weeks down the road, Joanna wants to come so she can meet her. It went EXACTLY as I imagined it would. The two Jo's hit it off and our friendship strengthened even more.

Through Jo, we'd meet a plethora of new friends over the years including her partner in crime, Susan. Time after time, we'd be impressed with their professionalism and down-home country spirit, which kept us coming back and itching for more.

I'll never forget the day we invited them to a Halloween party at our house. They didn't think it was real. That people you only speak to while at work would invite you to their home. But, against their better judgment, they showed up.

Not only did they show up, but they showed up with gratitude. And this time, we got to brag about them and introduce the two of them to all of our friends.

Days turn into weeks, weeks turn into months, and months turn into years. Now, nearly eight years later, this single moment in a parking lot showed me the kind of person Jo was, and it has led to her being one of my most trusted friends.

Jo speaks her mind and shares her faith like there's no tomorrow. She's inquisitive about everything happening around her and asks thought-provoking questions regularly.

It would have been easy to overlook someone like Jo and merely say she was "doing her job." If I had, I would have missed out on thousands of interactions that have made my life so much better in more ways than I can count.

Jo shines when the world gets dim. She lights other candles when they go out. And she guards hers with all her might as she knows how important it is.

Past that, Jo is the epitome of what excellent customer service should look like and the kind of friend we all need in our lives. Pay attention to those around you who treat others well for no reason at all. They're the good ones.

Oh, and to simply say Jo is "outstanding in her field" would be a major understatement... but it's a good start.

MAKING IT MATTER

Essence of the Moment

True connections can emerge in the most unexpected places, transforming routine encounters into lifelong friendships. When we take time to notice and nurture these moments, they have the power to truly brighten our lives.

Timeless Truths

- ☑ **Kindness Leaves a Mark:** Small, genuine gestures of care can create lasting impressions.
- ☑ **Friendship Knows No Bounds:** A single interaction can evolve into a bond that spans years and transforms lives.
- ☑ **Shine Where You Stand**: Bringing light to others, even in simple ways, can make a profound difference.

Bringing It Home

1. **Recognize Genuine Connections:** Think about your interactions today. Is there someone who consistently brings positivity or goes above and beyond? Take a moment to acknowledge their kindness, even if it's just a quick "thank you" or a small gesture of gratitude.
2. **Deepen Relationships:** This week, reach out to someone whose presence has impacted you. It could be a colleague, a neighbor, or even a barista who always brightens your mornings. Let them know their efforts matter and bring joy to others.
3. **Celebrate Your Jo:** By the end of the month, find a way to honor someone who consistently uplifts others. Plan a small gathering, write a heartfelt note, or simply tell them what they mean to you. Celebrate their impact on your life.

Next Level Thinking

Ask yourself:

▷ Have I overlooked someone's kindness simply because it felt "routine"?

▷ What can I do to amplify the light someone else shines in the world?

▷ How do I ensure my own actions reflect the kind of kindness and authenticity I admire in others?

▷ Who in my life might need a little encouragement to keep spreading their own light?

Insight to Remember

"Pay attention to those around you who treat others well for no reason at all. They're the good ones."

34

SEND AND RECEIVE

Was it the moment I hit "send" or the moment she responded? Either way, an exciting new world opened before me, and I had no idea what to expect. All thanks to my friend Dan, who, with his usual mix of humor and encouragement, nudged me out of my comfort zone and into a conversation with someone I'd never met.

Her name was Jennifer, and though I knew her only through her words, something about how she expressed herself drew me in —it was sharp, thoughtful, and layered with a kind of quiet confidence that made you want to know more.

Still, I hesitated. Would she be the same in real life? Would the depth of her words match the person in my mind?

I second-guessed every word of my message. I wrote, deleted, and wrote again—over and over. Finally, I took a deep breath and hit "send."

Jennifer's response came quickly, and with it, a smile emerged. Her curiosity and openness were evident, even in those first few exchanges. One conversation turned into ten, and soon, we planned to meet in person.

I was nervous. Not because I doubted her but because I doubted anyone could be as authentic in person as they were in writing. Within ten minutes, I had my answer.

Jennifer was every bit as genuine, insightful, and engaging as her words suggested—if not more so. Meeting her felt less like an introduction and more like reconnecting with someone I'd known for years.

Day after day, our conversations deepened. We talked about everything—our careers, our aspirations, the people who had shaped us, and the impact we wanted to have on the world. She had a way of making big ideas feel personal and actionable, and every discussion left me with something new to think about.

Then, one day, Jennifer asked me a question that changed everything: "Have you ever thought about working with engineers?"

It seemed random at first, but she quickly clarified. "At Raytheon, I mean. My dad's an engineer there, and I think you'd be a great fit."

The idea had never crossed my mind, but what she said with it made me believe it was possible. "The way you think, the questions you ask, how logical you are—oh my gosh, you'd love it!"

She didn't just float the idea—she championed me. "I'll tell him all about you," she said confidently, leaving no room for doubt.

Introductions were made, interviews followed, and soon, I found myself immersed in a world I hadn't anticipated but was more than ready to embrace. Her belief in me had opened a door I didn't know existed.

But Jennifer's impact didn't stop there. Over time, she became more than a friend—she became a trusted advisor and a connector of people. Qualities that, to this day, I try to emulate. She introduced me to her network, each connection as thoughtfully made as the last.

A few mentionable ones include Rose and Mindy, the CPAs who brought clarity to the chaos of numbers once we started our business. Then, the trademark and copyright attorneys who helped me protect what mattered most. And then she introduced me to Mark—her stepfather, who came into my life with a quiet wisdom and a heart of service.

Mark was more than just a sales manager—he was a mentor, a sounding board, and, in many ways, a kindred spirit. While our paths didn't align for us to work together professionally, his influence left a lasting impression.

He became a friend to my family, a supporter of my daughters' golf pursuits, and someone I could count on for advice that was always practical and deeply kind—including his push for me to write books. Over the years, I've engaged with him hundreds of times and have enjoyed watching him work with veterans and help set up Honor Flights.

Jennifer, meanwhile, continues to inspire me with her thoughtfulness and creativity. Her handwritten notes of thank-you's, encouragements, and reminders of the good in the world are small but powerful gestures that reflect who she is at the core.

Even today, her notes have become my benchmark for crafting meaningful thoughts in ways that genuinely connect with people.

And Dan, the friend who started it all, reminded me of the importance of stepping out of our comfort zones—and he still does. Without his nudge, I never would have sent that first message. I never would have met Jennifer or Mark. I never would have experienced the cascade of moments that followed.

Looking back, it's clear how much of life hinges on a single decision, a single conversation, or a single act of courage. For me, that decision was hitting "send." It was a small act, but it set in motion a series of connections that changed my trajectory in ways I couldn't have imagined.

Jennifer showed me what it means to believe in others and to share the world you've built with someone you trust. Dan reminded me that the most powerful moments often begin with a leap of faith. And Mark embodied the kind of quiet, steadfast leadership that leaves a lasting impact.

Together, they taught me that the right people, at the right time, can change everything—not just in the big, dramatic ways, but in the small, meaningful moments that shape who we are. And for that, I will always be grateful.

MAKING IT MATTER

Essence of the Moment

A single act of courage can spark connections that ripple through our lives, creating opportunities, lessons, and friendships that define us. It's often the small moments that lead to the most significant transformations.

Timeless Truths

- ☑ **Courage Creates Connections:** Stepping outside your comfort zone can lead to relationships and opportunities you never imagined.
- ☑ **Trust Sparks Growth:** Believing in others and sharing your network can unlock potential in ways that benefit everyone.
- ☑ **Generosity Fosters Meaningful Relationships:** Offering your time, advice, or support builds stronger bonds and creates lasting impacts on those around you.

Bringing It Home

1. **Lean Into Courage:** Have you hesitated to reach out to someone or take a bold step? Before the day ends, send that message, make that call, or take the leap. You never know what it might set in motion.
2. **Foster Growth Through Connections:** Take a moment this week to connect two people in your network who could benefit from knowing each other. Whether it's a shared skill set or common goals, your introduction might open doors for both.
3. **Celebrate Thoughtful Gestures:** By the month's end, make a list of people who have influenced your journey. Write a note, send an email, or make a call to let them know how they've impacted your life. Small acts of gratitude can deepen those bonds.

Next Level Thinking

Ask yourself:
- ▷ How often do I hesitate out of fear, and what opportunities might I be missing as a result?
- ▷ When was the last time I truly believed in someone and championed their growth?
- ▷ Who in my life could benefit from a thoughtful connection, and how can I facilitate that?
- ▷ What small, consistent actions can I take to express my gratitude and nurture my relationships?

Insight to Remember

"The right people, at the right time, can change everything—not just in the big, dramatic ways, but in the small, meaningful moments that shape who we are."

35

DUCT-TAPE DREAMS

Can an empty tent launch dreams and transform lives? It can, but only if your name is DD and you sign up for a random craft show on a whim.

Nope, this wasn't just any ordinary craft show—it was for antiques... and uniques. Nor was it for her—it was for three young ladies. And she was about to tell them.

"Oh, you'll never believe what I signed you girls up for!" DD beamed with excitement, the way only she could.

The three young ladies are sisters. By young, we're talking nine and younger. McKenzie, Breanna, and Kelbie—and they were artists in the making with entrepreneurial spirits.

"Oooh, yay!! You mean we get to sell these? We have to start making more!" McKenzie blurted out as she took off towards the art room.

"We'll need a sign... and a way to display things... and chairs. Wait, what are we gonna call ourselves? Oh, and we'll need price tags—how much are we gonna charge, Dad?"

For months, they'd been perfecting their craft of duct-tape wallets, accessories, and decorations. Every bit of hard work would be on display, and this time, it would pay off. "Again, what are we calling ourselves?" one of them asked.

They needed a name.

After hours of brainstorming, they figured out a way to combine their three names and locked it in... *Kenziannagrace.*

"Kenzi-anna-grace. KENZIANNAGRACE. I love it!" DD said, wide-mouthed and eyebrows raised, practicing it like a proud spokesperson.

The week leading up to the show was a whirlwind. Dozens of duct tape rolls filled our living room with prototypes all set out for critique and refinement. Conversations on the daily flowed with equal parts excitement and nerves.

DD was there every step of the way, offering tips and cheering them on while they prepared.

"Do you think we'll sell anything?" Mckenzie said with a hint of worry.

Breanna grinned. "What if we make a hundred bucks?"

The night before the show, they did a full dress rehearsal. They set their inventory up, practiced their sales pitches, and worked on how to greet people. They were a funny mix of both nervous and excited!

Morning came, and the girls were up and buzzing before the bees. A light breakfast, a quick car loading, and a final check of outfits—we were well on our way.

"I'm so excited," exclaimed McKenzie from the backseat.

DD was already at the tent when we arrived at the show, talking with vendors and strategizing. The moment she spotted the girls, a switch was flipped, and her demeanor shifted into high gear.

"These are my beautiful granddaughters," she'd announce to anyone passing by, "and they made every single one of these by hand. Aren't they amazing?"

Some people are passive at events and just wait for interest—not DD. She stood there, loud and proud, and actively drew people in. "Have you ever seen such creative wallets? Which one's your favorite? Let me show you this design over here... isn't it clever?"

Customers flocked to their tent, charmed as much by DD's enthusiasm as by the girls and their creations. With every customer, their confidence grew, their conversations improved, and their chins lifted.

"This is so much fun," said Kelbie, "and the people are so nice!"

By the end of the event, they had sold several hundred dollars worth of inventory, and they were over the moon with their first show. There was no doubt that they would figure out a way to keep their business going and try again.

But the real story wasn't the money.

DD's larger-than-life presence had given them an excellent role model to follow while showing them what it's like to have someone fully supporting you in the best ways possible. By cheering them on, building them up, and celebrating their wins WITH them.

That day did something for DD, too. It lit a fire where one was struggling to catch. She saw firsthand how much her encouragement boosted the girls' confidence, and from that day forward, she made it her mission to show up for them in every way possible. Golf tournaments, fundraisers, school projects—you name it, she was there!

Her involvement deepened after she married Scott, a man who not only supported her enthusiasm, but amplified it. Together, they'd show up, prioritize time with the kids, and find ways to surprise them with meaningful support.

Years later, at Breanna's high school graduation party, everyone was there except for DD and Scott, as they were 750 miles away.

"Knock, knock."

"Who's there?"

Ha. No joke here—it was DD and Scott. "Surprise!" They came, ready to celebrate, armed with hugs, smiles, and gifts. The moment they walked in, the air changed, and the party ramped up quickly.

For DD, it was never just about showing up—it was showing up with a purpose. It's who she is. From that first craft fair to that unexpected knock at the party, she's been a living example of what it means to love and support others wholeheartedly.

But it all started with an empty tent, a vision, and a chance.

That single decision wasn't just about selling duct-tape creations—it was about planting seeds. And watering them. It was about showing three young girls what they were capable of and proving how far love, encouragement, and showing up can take you in this world.

Sometimes, it takes just one person to see the best in us. To push, support, and remind us of what we're capable of when we step into the light.

For my girls, that person is DD.

And if you're lucky enough to have someone like her in your life, don't just thank them. Be like them. Because there's no shortage of people in this world who could use someone like you to believe in them.

MAKING IT MATTER

Essence of the Moment

It's not just about showing up—it's about showing up with purpose. Encouragement and love can spark confidence, ignite passions, and create ripple effects that last a lifetime.

Timeless Truths

- ☑ **Encouragement Changes Lives:** Belief and support from others can transform doubt into confidence and dreams into reality.
- ☑ **Purposeful Presence Matters:** Showing up with intention makes a more profound impact than mere attendance ever could.
- ☑ **Plant Seeds of Potential:** Even small actions of support can help others grow into who they're meant to be.

Bringing It Home

1. **Show Up Fully:** Next time you're asked to support someone, think beyond just attending. Is there a way to actively encourage, guide, or celebrate them? Take today to write down three people you could champion in small, meaningful ways.
2. **Speak with Enthusiasm:** Make it a point to speak with genuine excitement when discussing someone's talents or

accomplishments this week. Highlight their strengths to others and let them see how much they're appreciated.

3. **Be the Unexpected Support:** Find a way to surprise someone with your presence or support by the end of the month. It could be attending their event, helping with a project, or just being there when they least expect it.

Next Level Thinking

Ask yourself:

- How often do I actively cheer on those I care about?
- Who has been a "DD" in my life, and how can I show them my gratitude?
- What would it look like for me to show up for someone in a way that surprises and uplifts them?
- How can I use my voice and presence to create lasting, positive impressions for those around me?

Insight to Remember

"Sometimes, it takes just one person to see the best in us. To push us, support us, and remind us of what we're capable of when we step into the light."

36

CHOOSING COMPASSION

September 11, 2001. A regular status meeting at Raytheon was interrupted by a knock at the door, bringing the first news of the Twin Towers.

The meeting was my team's regular status meeting. Lt. Col. Cash was running the show, and all the regulars were there. We were discussing upgrades on secure telecommunication networks when the interruption came in.

I spent the next couple of hours in the lunchroom watching the events unfold on TV. There were hundreds of other engineers, program managers, and support staff.

The room was electrified with emotion—you could feel it in the air. Questions stirred: "What does this mean for our country?" "What will happen next?" "Who's responsible for this?" "Are we going to be okay?"

Yet, in the absence of answers, something remarkable happened: people connected. Strangers shared stories, offered support, hugged one another, and displayed a level of humanity I hadn't seen before.

That evening, my world shifted again.

I was on a date with Kristen, a young lady I had been seeing casually. We ended up at a sports bar where the TV played clips of the day's devastation on a loop. As I tried to process everything and talk with her about it, her reaction stunned me:

"It doesn't affect me at all," she said, in the most dismissing and nonchalant way. "Sucks for them, but I couldn't care less."

Her apathy left me speechless. The day's events had revealed the best in so many people, and yet here I was, having dinner with someone who seemed completely unfazed by it all.

Later that night, Joanna called. Weeks earlier, I had broken things off with her to "figure things out." We were still talking, but it wasn't exclusive. As I said goodnight to Kristen to take the call, I didn't realize that conversation would change my life.

Joanna asked me how I was holding up and shared her thoughts about the day. Her voice was full of compassion—to the extent that it was touching.

She spoke about the families affected, the bravery of first responders, and the resilience she hoped the country would show. She listened intently as I shared my own thoughts, asking questions and encouraging me to open up.

Her empathy was the missing ingredient I hadn't realized I needed. I saw what I couldn't before: that caring is a must-have quality for me regarding relationships.

Someone who doesn't just hear you but listens. Someone who offers something greater than just understanding—perspective.

Before I went to bed that night, I realized who I wanted to spend my life with. I called Joanna back the next day and began working to rebuild what we had already started.

I proposed just over three months later, and six months after that, we were married. Everyone in that meeting with me at Raytheon attended the wedding and cheered us on.

The events of 9/11 taught me that life is fragile and fleeting, but that wasn't my only takeaway. That day also showed me that who we share our lives with matters deeply. Joanna reminded me that compassion, connection, and shared humanity are true foundations of a meaningful life.

Moments like 9/11 may bring people together, but the small, everyday conversations show us who truly matters. When the smoke cleared that day, my path forward became clear: I wanted a life built on compassion, and that's precisely what I found with Joanna.

MAKING IT MATTER

Essence of the Moment

In a world shaken by tragedy, showing compassion and connecting with others becomes our greatest strength. It's what defines the relationships that truly matter.

Timeless Truths

- ☑ **Compassion Reveals Character:** How we respond to others' pain says more about us than our words ever could.
- ☑ **Humanity is Found in Connection:** In the face of adversity, shared empathy and understanding build bridges we didn't know we needed.
- ☑ **Small Moments Matter:** Life's most meaningful decisions are often shaped by quiet, heartfelt conversations.

Bringing It Home

1. **Lead with Empathy:** When someone shares their struggles, be present and intentional. Today, take a moment to really listen to someone, whether it's over coffee or a quick phone call, and let them feel heard.
2. **Create Space for Connection:** Think about a person who may need encouragement this week. It could be a coworker, friend, or even a stranger. Reach out with a small, thoughtful gesture that reminds them they're not alone.
3. **Build on the Everyday Moments:** Find a way to strengthen your most important relationship by the end of the month. It could be a handwritten note, a meaningful conversation, or simply carving out uninterrupted time to be together.

Next Level Thinking

Ask yourself:

▷ When was the last time I truly connected with someone without distraction?

▷ How do I show compassion daily, even when it's inconvenient?

▷ Who in my life has demonstrated empathy and care, and how can I express gratitude for them?

▷ How can I ensure the relationships I value most are nurtured and not taken for granted?

Insight to Remember

"Moments like 9/11 may bring people together, but it's the small, everyday conversations that show us who truly matters."

37

THE WELCOMING PARTY

We were in the clubhouse talking with the club Pro and his assistant about signing up. Joanna, the kids, and I were on the fence, asking questions better suited for someone else.

Well, that someone just happened to be a one-person welcoming party, and she walked in on her day off—right then and there. Purely accidental. Or was it?

Within seconds of seeing and meeting us, her smile became fully engaged, her eyes opened with excitement, and her hand was outstretched and ready to welcome us.

She even took the time to learn each of our kid's names.

That was a little over eight years ago.

At the time, she was working for a country club a good forty or so miles from us and was doing the marketing for them. She impressed us that day with how personable she was and how attentive to details she could be.

We hit it off with her as a family, and everyone always asked about her when we visited.

As life moves on, so do people. People come and go in jobs, in towns, in friendships, and in general, and others stay connected for some reason or another.

Sometimes, that reason is because they're good people, and you want to keep them around.

This particular lady moved on but kept us in the loop, and we kept her in ours. As my kids got older, so did hers. We parented together, separately, and always made the time to say hello through online posts and through Messenger. Occasionally, we'd see her in person, and it was just like old times.

I've watched this mom participate in her kids' lives, stand up for her kids and others in ways most people won't, lobby for changes, voice her opinions, help others, and love on her community.

More than anyone I know, she promotes businesses her friends run, places she frequents, and programs around her to help spread the word for them. She's a real-life rockstar regarding promotions and getting people excited.

She spends so much time helping others and does it because building community is essential to her. She and I sat and had coffee a few months back and had a wonderful conversation about this very thing.

Day in and day out, she impresses me with her resilience and willingness to keep getting up after being knocked down.

Oh, and I've witnessed firsthand how big of a heart this incredible lady has. I'll never forget how sweet and kind she was while taking McKenzie's first prom pictures and what she did as a surprise for Breanna's 16th birthday, as she's a fantastic photographer.

For all these reasons, I called her out in the front of my last book, but I knew she needed her own chapter where her story fits a little too perfectly.

So, if you're reading this and anywhere near Somerset, KY, hit her up the next time you need a personable photographer you'll just adore—her name is Amanda. Amanda Muse. And her page on Facebook is Soulful Studios LLC.

Thank you, Amanda, for welcoming us the way you did, for all you do for your community, and for lighting the way for others to shine.

MAKING IT MATTER

Essence of the Moment

True community builders don't just create connections—they inspire others to do the same. Amanda's warmth and genuine care remind us that making people feel seen and valued changes everything.

Timeless Truths

- ☑ **Kindness Creates Bonds:** Simple gestures of kindness have the power to build connections that last a lifetime.
- ☑ **Promote Others' Success:** Amplifying the efforts of others strengthens communities and relationships.
- ☑ **Resilience Inspires Action:** Those who keep going despite challenges set an example for others to follow.

Bringing It Home

1. **Make the First Move:** When you meet someone new, find a way to make them feel genuinely welcome—maybe it's a smile, remembering their name, or asking about their story. A small act today could start a meaningful connection.
2. **Celebrate Others:** This week, use your platform—whether it's social media or a face-to-face interaction—to promote someone else's work or passion. Sharing their success can ripple through your community.
3. **Grow Your Community:** By the end of the month, make a plan to deepen a connection you already have. Maybe it's grabbing coffee with someone inspiring or volunteering alongside them. Strengthen your ties to the people who matter most.

Next Level Thinking

Ask yourself:

- How often do I take the time to genuinely welcome someone into my life or space?
- When was the last time I celebrated someone else's success, and how did it impact them—and me?
- What steps can I take to better support the people in my community?
- Am I consistently surrounding myself with people who inspire me to grow and give back?

Insight to Remember

"More than anyone I know, she promotes businesses her friends run, places she frequents, and programs around her to help spread the word for them. She's a real-life rockstar when it comes to promotions and getting people excited."

38

THE HAIL MARY

Every father wants his daughter's sixteenth birthday to be special, right? Well, I'm no exception.

As fate would have it, my firstborn's sixteenth would fall smack in the middle of the first year of the pandemic.

Not good.

The world was confused. People were hiding and scared. Businesses were shut down, and masks were being worn.

We came to the realization about three weeks prior to her birthday that we weren't going to have a party after all. No celebrations with other people. No going out anywhere. No having anyone over.

She was heartbroken. To the extent that I was genuinely concerned.

About two weeks before her birthday, I was nervous. I didn't have any kind of a plan that would be remotely helpful as it related to something we could do for her.

Then I threw a Hail Mary, hoping someone on my team would catch it.

My team consisted of all sorts of talented players. Players from Florida, Georgia, California, North Carolina, Utah, Nevada, New York, Oklahoma, Pennsylvania, Maryland, Alabama, Kentucky, and Tennessee. Just to name a few.

The Hail Mary was a post where I blocked my daughter, explained the situation, and asked for help. It was all in the hopes of making her sixteenth something memorable.

I didn't expect what happened next.

Three days before her birthday, the letters and boxes started arriving. Two days before, there was even more, and the mailman had to come drop them off at the house because the mailbox was full. The day before, more again. And the day of, it was madness.

My daughter, who knew nothing about this, was in complete shock when she came into our kitchen that day and saw that it was loaded with the most beautiful gifts and cards.

Nearly a hundred and fifty friends of ours took time out of their lives to ensure my daughter didn't feel neglected. Now, I don't know if you've ever tried to open a hundred and fifty items for your birthday, but it's overwhelming... to say the least.

One by one, she opened them and took in their messages. "You don't know me, but...," "I can't wait to one day meet you...," "I know what it's like to...," and, "Your dad told me all about..."

Some of the most beautiful hand-written cards you could imagine were a part of the collection. Heartfelt, meaningful, and relevant to the time we were living through.

I watched and sat with her that day while telling her stories about each of the people who were friends of mine. And Joanna told the stories of her friends.

Her "moment" lasted for hours. Shock, laughter, and tears were all regularly seen. Gift cards, handmade gifts, cash, and practical items filled the gap where I thought the emptiness would be, and it was nothing short of amazing.

I'll never know what drove people to action that day, but I can tell you that the magic happened. A community of people stepped up and did something without anyone noticing, all to ensure a young lady didn't feel neglected.

It turns out that moments like this are not only special—they're what every father dreams of. That day, my dreams came true because I got to see the true power of community and what it means to help each other out.

Oh, and I should mention this, too. Over the next week, I watched my daughter's gratitude get the best of her. She hand-painted and then hand-wrote and sent a hundred-and-fifty thank you cards. One to each and every person. To ensure that they didn't feel neglected either.

As for who caught the Hail Mary pass? Everyone. It was quite the scene.

MAKING IT MATTER

Essence of the Moment

Sometimes, a little effort and a community's generosity can transform disappointment into joy. When the right people are involved, the simplest ask can create unforgettable moments of connection and gratitude.

Timeless Truths

- ☑ **The Power of Asking:** A sincere request can inspire an extraordinary response.
- ☑ **Community Matters:** True connection shines brightest during challenging times.
- ☑ **Gratitude Multiplies Joy:** Expressing thanks can deepen the meaning of any gesture.

Bringing It Home

1. **Create a Ripple:** Think about someone in your life who could use a little extra encouragement. Whether it's a quick note, a small gift, or just a thoughtful check-in, take a moment today to reach out.

2. **Celebrate Togetherness:** Find a way to bring your community closer this week, even if it's virtual. Start a group message, organize a small gathering, or simply share something that lifts everyone's spirits.
3. **Show Your Gratitude:** Take time before the month ends to write a heartfelt thank-you to someone who has impacted your life. Be specific, and let them know how much they mean to you.

Next Level Thinking

Ask yourself:
▷ Have I recently asked for help when I needed it, or do I let pride get in the way?
▷ Who in my community could benefit from a little unexpected kindness right now?
▷ How can I make gratitude a more consistent practice in my daily life?
▷ What am I doing to nurture the connections that matter most to me?

Insight to Remember

"Moments like this are not only special—they're what every father dreams of. That day, my dreams came true because I got to see the true power of community and what it means to help each other out."

39

QUICK-CONNECTS

The rains had moved in, and our morning was shot. We were only a few days into our largest contract and wanted to use the time wisely. So my son suggests we go back to where he got degreaser a couple of days earlier and insists that I go in with him.

It's not that he's incapable of it—it was more that he wanted me to see the inside. "They have everything in there, Dad!" he said.

We pulled up, and I took it in. It was very unassuming. An old sign. Small parking lot. Average curb appeal. Messaging that didn't exactly tell me what I was stepping into. Underwhelming, at best.

"Do I have to?" I said.

"Dad, come on. You'll be surprised."

So I went in. And surprised I was. We were greeted almost immediately by Lori and Diane, two ladies who looked like they could be sisters. My son asked for the bathroom and promptly left. Now, it's just me and these two, and they're wondering what they can help me with.

I have questions—loads of questions. They have answers—witty and comical answers. My son returns, gets in on it, and then takes the questions to a whole new level.

In an instant, the mannerisms of these two change. They're intrigued. They ask about my son's age, and when they find out, they are blown away by his knowledge, insight, and demeanor.

Over the next couple of hours, they learned about the business he was setting up and helped him like he was their own. I just got to sit back and watch the magic happen.

We heard stories of their business, of competitors, and of grease hoods. We talked about surface cleaners, soft-washing, and nozzles. Then, it turned to business insurance, and they went as far as to call several of their customers to ask who they use and who they recommend.

It was a masterclass in professionalism and generosity. These two ladies wanted to see my son succeed and not make the same mistakes others make.

And he was listening—oh, was he ever. He was grinning ear-to-ear and eating it up. Bite-size chunk after bite-size chunk was devoured like he was at a buffet.

Diane took over for the last half-hour and walked him through all sorts of professional options. Then, when he made his selection of things he needed now, she asked if there was anything else. At this point, he only had a downstream injector and felt good about it. After thinking briefly, he decided it would be best to have a couple of quick connects, and she made it happen.

"Anything else?"

"No ma'am. We got way more out of this than we expected, and I'm super excited about what you shared with me."

Well, it got better. About the time he went to pay, Diane tells him it's all taken care of. No charge whatsoever.

My son's face was a weird combination of excitement and shock. About the same as what theirs was when they found out his age. And he was so gracious with his response that he managed to get some hugs out of the deal.

Diane says she was impressed with his questions and work ethic and wanted him to remember that some people still notice and care.

All of it matters because none of it had to happen. The two ladies could have just been order takers, but they were anything but. They could have ignored us and not engaged, but they chose to absolutely delight us with their service.

And the unexpected connection, kindness, and mentorship? Priceless.

If you ever need pressure washing products, please look them up. They're in Clearwater, FL, but they do a ton of business online. Their business name is Pressure Washer Service, Inc. , and their website is pressurewasherproducts (dot com). Ask for Lori or Diane and tell them how much you appreciate how they treated young Mr. Trautman and how they made a lasting impact on his dad.

So, again, a couple of takeaways to remember. Don't judge a book by its cover. Give people and stores a chance. Let people be people and do their thing. And stay and hang with people who are good conversationalists—they're worth your time and what I'll now call Quick-Connects!

How fitting!

MAKING IT MATTER

Essence of the Moment

Sometimes, the most unexpected places and people can offer the greatest connections. Genuine kindness and thoughtful mentorship can transform a simple errand into a life-changing experience.

Timeless Truths

- ☑ **Authenticity Stands Out:** Genuine care and attention create memorable interactions that leave a lasting impression.
- ☑ **Mentorship Matters:** Sharing knowledge freely can empower others and spark meaningful growth.
- ☑ **Kindness is Contagious:** Generosity inspires gratitude and motivates others to pay it forward.

Bringing It Home

1. **Keep an Open Mind:** Next time you're hesitant about visiting a place or meeting someone new, take a chance. You might discover something—or someone—that surprises you in the best possible way.
2. **Create a Meaningful Connection:** When engaging with others this week, go beyond the surface. Ask thoughtful questions, listen actively, and see where the conversation takes you.
3. **Pay It Forward:** Before the month ends, find a way to help someone without expecting anything in return. Whether it's advice, encouragement, or a small gesture, make it count for someone who'll never forget it—just like Diane did.

Next Level Thinking

Ask yourself:
- When was the last time I judged a situation or person too quickly, and how can I avoid doing that again?
- How can I make a more deliberate effort to connect with others and learn from their expertise?
- What small act of generosity can I offer that might greatly impact someone's life?
- Who has shown me an unexpected kindness, and how can I express my gratitude or pass it on?

Insight to Remember

"Don't judge a book by its cover. Give people and stores a chance. Let people be people and do their thing. And stay and hang with people that are good conversationalists."

40

ONE

It just takes one. One. Not ten. Not a hundred. Not EVERY one of them. Who? Your friends. It just takes one.

One. One friend. Someone to be accountable to. Someone who you know you've made a commitment to and that you'll see it through.

Because not seeing it through means your word doesn't mean anything.

Accountability provides the "why" when you can't justify anything else. Accountability says we know and understand what we signed up for, and we're willing to see it through. Accountability says you'll do something even though you can't see the benefits quite yet. Accountability says you're responsible for what you say and agree to and that you do it.

A few months back, I listened to a friend's request. His name is James, and he's self-proclaimed "not a reader."

He asked that I "read" my leadership book aloud so he could listen while he worked. I laughed. He laughed. I asked if he was serious. He said he was.

Then, he asked me to read a chapter out loud to him over the phone—for real. I laughed. He laughed. I asked if he was serious. He said he was.

I did. I fumbled. I re-read several lines to "get them right." I laughed at my own "reading" and apologized for "not getting it right the first time."

Then, something happened.

He said, "I'm not even kidding—hearing you read it is SO much better than my interpretation of it."

He then asked if I could read and record the whole thing. I laughed. He laughed. Then it went silent. "Really," he said.

It was at that moment I knew. I had a reason to do something I didn't want to do. To learn a skill on something I felt I was terrible at. To work through all the backend data I didn't know how to do. To cringe my way through the editing. To figure out how to actually get it done.

And so I gave him my word that I'd do it.

Take by take, I worked my way through. I fumbled. I hiccuped. I struggled. I got mad. But I kept going. Until I liked it. Until it made sense. Until I smiled. Until I got it right. And, one by one, I'd send him chapters. Completed.

And that's what accountability does. It forces us to stand up when we want to sit. It gets us to swing when we want to hold back. It tells us to keep going when we want to quit.

I stood. I swung. I kept going. Six-thousand one-hundred and thirty-five takes, but you know what? I found my voice and finished my first audiobook—because of my word.

Accountability.

Whatever you want to do in this world, make it known. Tell someone. Give someone your word. Do what you say. Get up when you want to sleep in. Do the "thing"—whatever the "thing" is. But more importantly, hold yourself accountable... to someone.

It just takes one.

MAKING IT MATTER

One commitment to the right person can create the accountability needed to achieve what seemed impossible. It's not about perfection—it's about staying true to your word and showing up.

Timeless Truths

- ☑ **Accountability Amplifies Effort:** Having someone you're answerable to can make all the difference in following through.
- ☑ **Your Word Defines You:** Following through on commitments shapes your character and builds trust.
- ☑ **Effort Creates Mastery:** Repetition and persistence can transform struggles into strengths.

Bringing It Home

1. **Reflect on Your Commitments:** Think about something you've promised to do but haven't yet tackled. Whether a simple task or a meaningful project, taking the first small step right now can feel empowering and move you closer to honoring your word.
2. **Strengthen a Connection:** Consider reaching out to someone who inspires or holds you accountable like James did. Share an update, ask for their perspective, or simply check in this week—building that connection could give you the push you need to stay on track.
3. **Set a Personal Goal:** As you look ahead over the next few weeks, identify a skill, habit, or project that's been on your mind. Make it a priority to work on it consistently and celebrate your progress, however small it may seem.

Next Level Thinking

Ask yourself:
- ▷ What's a goal I've been procrastinating on because I feel stuck or unmotivated?
- ▷ Who could be the "one" to help hold me accountable, and how can I involve them?
- ▷ How does accountability change my approach to challenges and follow-through?
- ▷ How can I pay it forward by being the "one" for someone else?

Insight to Remember

"Whatever you want to do in this world, make it known. Tell someone. Give someone your word. Do what you say. Get up when you want to sleep in. Do the "thing"—whatever the "thing" is. But more importantly, hold yourself accountable... to someone."

41

JACK IN THE BACK

Here I am in a large country nightclub. I'm teaching a line dance class with easily two hundred fifty students. It's dark, crowded, loud, and shoulder-to-shoulder with an eclectic group of enthusiastic people all there to get their *dance on*.

Step-by-step, we're all making progress and working our way through the dance. I hear the regular clapping bits, laughing fits, an occasional groan, and a lot of small talk accompanied by feet shuffling and boots stomping.

This particular night, I'm teaching an intermediate-level line dance. I was nearing the end of the lesson, and then...

It happened.

We finished what we were working on, and I told everyone to face forward to start over from the top.

A guy named Jack (I know his name because he came and talked to me afterward) from the back of the dance floor yelled something that absolutely stopped me dead in my tracks.

I've replayed that moment probably a thousand times in my life, and it's been a guiding light for me ever since.

It's a perspective shift I now use while teaching in person, in writing, and on video.

I'll share what "Jack in the back" said in a moment, but first, there's something else you should know.

It's natural for most people to look for a reason they can't do something. "He goes too fast," or "She goes too slow," or "They're just not good at explaining things," or, my favorite, "It's just too confusing for me."

Pronouns also get people riled up.

No, not those kinds of pronouns, but these... "this," "that," and "the other," as in... use this hand, step that way, or now step with the other foot.

Here's where it matters.

If you were to close your eyes and I tell you to "Put this hand on your hip," you'd immediately say, "Which hand AND which hip?"... right?

If you didn't, we probably can't be friends.

Now, let's revisit our friend Jack from earlier. I had just used this exact phrase, "Okay, now, everyone face forward."

Yeah, well, "Jack in the back" yelled out, "WE'RE ALWAYS FACING FORWARD!"

Seems silly, but it isn't.

It hit me like a ton of bricks. I had no comeback nor witty response whatsoever. Everyone heard it. Everyone laughed. I just stood there for a couple of seconds and processed what he said with a perplexed look.

From that perspective, Jack was absolutely right.

I had just used words that left people confused and it made a lasting impression on me like very few moments do in our lives.

You see, using a specific point of reference is critical. Using phrases like "this hand," "the other foot," "turn around," "like this," "face forward," or "do what I'm doing" are killers in a dance class.

I should have known better, but it took THAT MOMENT to teach me. It made such an impact on how I speak to people, how I write materials, and how I give directions.

I literally think through my words as though I'm telling someone who's blind.

And, I've now taken it a bit further if I'm teaching something and I test material out to people with their eyes closed. I try to be as clear as I can be with my words so that it makes sense as a standalone piece.

I regularly ask these questions: "Am I communicating what this person needs to do and to think about at the right time?" and "Are the words I'm using clear enough for anyone to follow?"

Today, I'd like you to think like "Jack in the back" and listen for specifics. Do yourself a favor and see what it's like to follow along with your eyes closed.

MAKING IT MATTER

Essence of the Moment

Even the smallest feedback can spark profound growth when we're open to it. Clarity in communication isn't just about speaking—it's about truly connecting with those who are listening.

Timeless Truths

☑ **Specific Words Lead to Specific Results:** Clear, precise language is key to ensuring your message is understood and actionable.

☑ **Feedback Is a Gift:** Sometimes, the most unexpected voices offer the insights we need to refine and improve.

☑ **Perspective Matters:** Seeing—or hearing—things from another's viewpoint can shift your understanding in transformative ways.

Bringing It Home

1. **Practice Giving Directions:** Choose a simple task, like explaining how to make a sandwich or find an item in your home, and try explaining it to someone as if they couldn't see. Pay attention to how specific you are and adjust as needed.
2. **Ask for Feedback:** At some point this week, share instructions or a process you regularly explain with someone who isn't

familiar with it. Ask them how easy it was to follow and where they felt lost or needed more detail. Use their feedback to refine and improve your communication skills.

3. **Build Awareness:** Over the next month, focus on how you phrase your messages—whether written or spoken. Make a conscious effort to use specific, clear language that leaves little room for ambiguity.

Next Level Thinking

Ask yourself:
- How often do I assume my instructions are clear without checking for understanding?
- When was the last time I actively sought feedback on how I communicate?
- What habits or phrases might unintentionally confuse others?
- How can I practice being more precise and empathetic in my daily conversations?

Insight to Remember

"Am I communicating what this person needs to do and to think about at the right time?"

42

THE WRITE WORDS

We were somewhere between Roatan and Belize, the Caribbean sun melting into the horizon, when my daughters came running, bursting with excitement. Not only had they met new friends, but they were from Australia—and they don't speak very much English.

There were three of them—two girls and a boy, in the same order and ages as our first three. Their names were Jennifer, Jessica, and Jeremy—and they were all gymnasts.

"Can they eat dinner with us tonight, Dad?" McKenzie asked while tugging at my shirt. "Jessica's my age, and I really like her."

We found the three of them a short while later and met their parents, Zoltan and Tunde. A half-hour after that, we invited their whole family to dinner with us.

"Table for eleven, please," I requested as we looked like one big happy family.

Three hours. That's how long we all sat and talked that evening. We were all so different and enamored by each other's stories.

Oh, and we figured out why they didn't speak English—it was a question Joanna and I wondered about. Our girls were wrong; they weren't from Australia—it was Austria.

Big aha moment for the girls on that one!

Over the next several days, we included their family in our every plan. They were learning and practicing English, and we were learning and practicing patience.

When the cruise ended, we saw the ten-hour gap before their flight as an opportunity to invite them to our house and the beach. Zoltan, the father, had never driven in America, so I let him drive our SUV to see how it was. He was ecstatic!

They left, and we gave them an open invite for the girls to come and stay with us anytime. We kept in touch for a couple of years and continually reminded them about the offer.

I'll never forget the day I received his email. "The girls are on their way and will arrive tomorrow at 11am. You'll have to pick them up."

My eyes bulged. Wait, what? "Joanna..." I called out, as I walked across the house with my laptop in my hands.

I quickly went through old emails and saw how we'd discussed it, but never with specifics. The translation, though, left things a little less clear.

"Here is flight information. The girls fly International First-Class," he said without hesitation. "You be there with I.D. to pick them up."

They were flying into Atlanta, Georgia. Almost six-hours away. And on Eastern time.

The next morning came early. We were off and running by 3:30 to allow for any hiccups. Hiccups happened, and we jogged into the airport at 11:15—just as they were being escorted out.

Literally, perfect timing.

Now, with no translator, I did my best to use short sentences and draw pictures with my hands or just simply point and grunt.

"Food. Eat. Hungry. You?" I sounded more like a caveman, but it got the job done.

At Cracker Barrel, I resorted to wild hand gestures, exaggerated nods, and overly simple phrases. "Burger. Eggs. Biscuits. Fruit."

The more I talked, the more they giggled and spoke to each other in German.

I had no information on these girls nor much to go on other than they were staying with us for a couple of weeks, yet here I was doing the best I could do.

"Are you allergic to anything?" I asked, knowing full well that there might not be comprehension.

By their looks, I could tell they didn't get it. I pulled out Google Translate and tried to read out the words, then finally let them read them for themselves.

"No. No, no, no. We no allergic anything."

Great. I proceeded with the meal and continued. I should note that I'd asked the father via email the day before, but he hadn't responded.

The girls ate a wide variety of foods for lunch, and just as we were paying the bill, I received a response from their dad. Part of the response was that they were allergic to three different things, two of which they'd just eaten.

I just sat there and stared at my screen, wondering what the next few hours would be like. After a quick close of my eyes and a deep breath later, I let them read what their dad had just written.

This was a tense moment.

They were reading words they didn't know yet and trying to translate. One would read while the other was typing. All the while, I'm thinking I'm about to have a major problem relating to throats swelling—or worse.

It took about a minute—a minute that felt like an eternity as my fate, and theirs, hung in the balance.

"My father no write," Jennifer says with a confident look on her face.

"Yes, your father did write that," I said as I showed her the email address to validate my concern.

"No... you no understand."

Correct, I didn't. This would be a common theme going forward. It was more like a comedy show.

"*My father no write!*" she says again, this time more emphatically. The awkward silence afterward made me think through it, and then, I got it: I was wrong about write, it was right—as in correct.

"My mother say we no allergy, we okay."

For the next three weeks we traveled, worked in the garden, cooked foods, and shopped. Their English improved, and their taste buds went from "Me no like" to "Me like, want more" very quickly.

Our basement turned into a gymnastics arena, our food budget went through the roof, and our ability to communicate with them went up tenfold. Oh, and they did cartwheels and handstands everywhere, often in the middle of conversations. In the evenings, the girls told stories of where they were from and what their days and summers were like.

Then, another email. Mom, Dad, and Jeremy were on their way and going to stay with us too. This, at the same time my parents showed up out of the blue, and another family was visiting.

We all learned so much about other cultures, communication, and commitments that we were actually sad when it came to an end.

As we said our goodbyes, Jessica hugged me tightly, her eyes filled with tears. "Thank you for everything," she said in a flawless English tone. "I learned so much—not just about America, but about family, and about myself."

The moment we met the Balazs family, we knew it would be special. And it was. To this day, we all keep in touch with each other and celebrate successes and birthdays regularly.

Six years after their visit, I received a message from the eldest, Jessica. She asked me if I could help her with a presentation she was giving for her English class.

For weeks, we talked face-to-face on FaceTime, where she worked on correctly pronouncing different words and adding facial expressions, pauses, and hand movements while she spoke. She was so much fun and was a quick study.

Once again, it was a fantastic transformation, and she shared her "results" with me after her presentation.

"It went really good. My teacher was very impressed, and she really liked my presentation," she wrote. "I can't thank you enough for helping me!"

She even told me she delivered the whole thing without notecards—and was the only one in the class to do so.

All this happened because of a chance meeting on a cruise ship and an invite—not just to dinner, but to a lifetime friendship. Seizing opportunities isn't for the faint of heart, but it is for those who are willing to bet on the power of human connection.

And I'll bet on that one all day long.

So, yeah, friendships can form in the strangest of circumstances and, sometimes, just out of the blue. Connection to other humans is essential, and nationality doesn't care when we lead with the heart. Communication is communication, even if you don't know the 'write' words.

MAKING IT MATTER

Essence of the Moment

True connection transcends language and cultural barriers, creating bonds that leave lasting impressions and opportunities to grow together. The heart speaks volumes when words fail.

Timeless Truths

- ☑ **Open Hearts Build Bridges:** Genuine kindness and openness pave the way for meaningful connections, regardless of language or cultural differences.
- ☑ **Learning Together Creates Growth:** Shared experiences, even when challenging, lead to mutual understanding, stronger bonds, and invaluable lessons.
- ☑ **Every Invitation Matters:** A simple invitation can spark lifelong friendships and open doors to extraordinary opportunities.

1. **Find a Connection Point:** The next time you meet someone new, especially if there's a language barrier, focus on finding one shared interest or experience to build your conversation around. This small step can make an immediate connection feel effortless.
2. **Explore a New Culture:** This week, take time to learn about a culture different from your own—whether through food, music, or even a local event. Let curiosity lead you to understanding.
3. **Celebrate Differences in Communication:** Over the next month or so, challenge yourself to connect with someone whose first language isn't your own. Practice patience, use gestures, or even learn a few key phrases in their language. Small efforts can lead to profound connections.

Next Level Thinking

Ask yourself:
- How often do I let language or cultural differences stop me from engaging with someone?
- What steps can I take to build stronger cross-cultural connections in my community?
- How can I show curiosity and respect when communicating with someone from a different background?
- How have relationships outside of my comfort zone enriched my perspective on life?

Insight to Remember

"Seizing opportunities isn't for the faint of heart, but it is for those who are willing to bet on the power of human connection."

43

BREWING CONNECTIONS

There was something different about them. The way they walked, talked, and presented themselves caught my attention, but the moment the barista brought them their coffee, it all changed.

It was an ordinary Friday at a small, local coffee shop. Sitting with my friends Pedro and Jhon (that's not a typo) like I did every week, I'd people-watch while we conversed. This, in a place where I often made observations about customer service, or the lack thereof.

I had told the story many times of the day when I was the only one in there, and I had ordered a black coffee. Thirty seconds later, the same young lady who had taken my order yelled out "Black Coffee" at the "Pick-Up" end of the bar. She had set the drink down and returned to whatever she was doing. I remember standing there wondering why she wouldn't have just handed it to me.

It was one of many times I'd noticed that no matter how many people came in, they just didn't seem to make people feel like they mattered. And that's why this next piece really caught my attention.

I had seen probably sixty people walk through that door throughout the morning—thousands over the course of months. Kids on their way to school, nurses on their way to work, churchgoers on their way to Bible Studies—they had all come through.

Then, these two walk in and out of the cold—dressed sharply and with a look of sophistication that stood out: the lady in slacks, a white blouse, and a fancy red vest; the man was tall and slender with a well-groomed white beard, glasses, and muted tan jacket and slacks.

Normal stuff—they stand in line, place their order, and then take a seat. Didn't think anything of it. I watched and listened as the other customers were all served at the "Pick-Up" end. Again, normal. Then, I saw something I'd never seen in all my time I'd been frequenting this place.

One of the baristas packaged their order up, walked past everyone else in the shop, and hand-delivered their drinks and a pastry to them with a greeting that blew me away.

"So good to see you Ms. Beverly—here's your coffee. And here you are, Wally!" as she graciously handed them their drinks and proceeded to ask how everything was going and what they'd been up to.

I was stunned. It was so simple and heartwarming, but it wasn't the norm. I wish it were, but it wasn't. I told my friends about what had just happened, and they were equally impressed. Then, it really started to get to me, and my mind wouldn't let it go.

There's a part of the movie Remember the Titans where Petey says to Sunshine, "It don't matter to me, you know... I just gotta know." That's pretty much how it went down when I walked over to their table. I just had to know who they were or why that happened.

"Oh I just love that they always bring us our coffees," she tells me in the most polite and welcoming way. She was sincere, and he nodded with approval of her answer.

"Ha!" I started to say, shaking my head in disagreement. "That's the first time in months they've EVER delivered coffee to anyone. What secret do you know about them that they're afraid of you sharing?"

Laughter ensued, and so did introductions.

For the next thirty-five minutes, I learned so much about the two of them—and them, me. They're both in their early 70's but don't look or act like it. Fit, sharp-as-a-tack, witty, and well-spoken. Not your everyday run-of-the-mill people, and I picked up on it immediately. The mere articulation of their words and thoughts was intriguing.

My favorite part about meeting them was their positivity. How they were just full of it—in a good way. Stories of how much they love Florida's beaches were straight out of a tourist center's dream. Tales of the folks at their church and how welcoming they were would make you think they're on commission.

Whatever it was they were selling, I was buying. Story after story I just sat there in awe. Within minutes of talking with them, I knew why the folks there thought so highly of them and brought their order—because it allowed them to feed off their personalities and help make their day.

They were great listeners, too. The kind where the people are engaged, ask great questions and make candid faces while you talk. It was so fun—and the conversations were the kind you'd love to have with everyone, except it rarely happens. Then, just like that, it ended as they rushed out after noticing they were nearly late for an appointment.

The following week, however, it picked right back up when they walked in, waved and pointed at me, and said, "Hey there, Shawn!!!" I watched again as they got their order delivered to them, but this time, it was to my table—where they were now sitting with me.

Ms. Beverly was the first to read one of my stories—one about "asteroids" (if you know, you know)—and she laughed hysterically, then had Wally read it. It was on!

Week after week we'd see each other and visit. They would update me on all that was going on in their world and I'd share about mine.

They once walked in on me just minutes after I'd written a heartfelt piece the day my eldest went off to college. I'll never forget how Ms. Beverly leaned in, put her arm around me, and softly said:

"Whatever it is, Shawn, it'll be okay. God is right there with you."

The emotions of the moment had all but crippled my voice and flooded my eyes, and yet, no judgment from either of them—just pure compassion, love, and understanding. They didn't know the situation, but they didn't need to. They hugged me, said they'd keep me in their prayers, and told me I was loved—and that was enough.

I learned more about them and their lives each time including all of what Ms. Beverly had done with Weight Watchers over the years and so many of the IT projects Wally had been a part of. I recently learned that Ms. Beverly used to teach sign language and that opened up whole new avenues of conversation.

Recently, when they came to visit one day while I was on travel, the conversation led to recent writings and it just so happened to be the day I'd finalized my cover for *The Power of Moments*. They were the first to see it and could not have been more excited. They even talked about the "moment" we met and how powerful it was for them—just like it was for me.

Ms. Beverly and Mr. Wally have brought great joy to my life— both of them in their own unique ways. They've shared perspectives I never could have dreamed of without them. I've laughed with them, shed tears with them, had coffee with them, and hugged them both—many times. All because of who they were and how they stood out.

They're the perfect reminder of how we reap what we sow. We get back what we put into this world. Without their positivity, they never would have had their order delivered—and I certainly wouldn't have noticed anything other than their outfits and probably would have just gone on with my day.

Well, that's one moment I don't want to take back. One that has enriched my life and given me access to two of the most authentic and kindest souls you could imagine—both in person and online. I'm thankful for having met them that day and for everything they do to make the world better for everyone they come in contact with.

Sometimes it pays to pause, notice and engage with the world around us—and, for the record, I was right—there was something different about them.

MAKING IT MATTER

Essence of the Moment

Authentic connections are sparked by small, intentional actions—like noticing, engaging, and embracing the uniqueness of others. These moments can turn strangers into lifelong friends.

Timeless Truths

- ☑ **Kindness Creates Ripples:** Small gestures of thoughtfulness can inspire connection and joy far beyond the moment.
- ☑ **Engage with Intention:** Noticing and acknowledging the people around you opens doors to meaningful relationships.
- ☑ **Be Present:** The power of a single moment lies in your willingness to pause, engage, and truly see the person in front of you.

Bringing It Home

1. **Start Small:** Practice being present in your interactions. Look for an opportunity today to compliment someone or ask a thoughtful question to spark a connection.
2. **Expand Your Network:** This week, intentionally strike up a conversation with someone you see regularly but haven't spoken to yet. It could be a barista, a coworker, or even a neighbor.
3. **Cultivate Positivity:** By the end of the month, make a habit of finding ways to brighten others' days. Whether through small acts of kindness, offering encouragement, or simply being a good listener, your efforts can have a ripple effect.

Next Level Thinking

Ask yourself:
- How can I create a welcoming atmosphere for others in my daily interactions?
- When was the last time I intentionally sought to connect with someone new?
- What traits or behaviors do I admire in others that I could emulate to strengthen my relationships?
- How can I show gratitude to those who've made a positive impact on my life?

Insight to Remember

"Sometimes it pays to pause, notice and engage with the world around us."

44

LIVING THE MESSAGE

The thing about Buc-ee's is it's never just a gas station—it's an experience.

On any given day, you'll find hundreds of people dancing their way through the crowd, with reasons for being there as varied as the items on their shelves.

And, sure, everyone has a story, but not everyone wears it like this guy.

There, in the middle of the crowd, a young man caught my attention. He had a grin a mile wide and a presence that said he knew who he was. On top of that, he had an energy about him that just drew me in and a shirt that caught me off-guard.

It read, "BE GOOD TO PEOPLE FOR NO REASON."

I read it as he passed and it just... well... made sense. And this guy was pulling it off effortlessly. No, not literally.

As I went to grab my coffee, I couldn't help but think about the words on his shirt. I thought about how common it was for people to BE GOOD TO PEOPLE FOR A REASON—like, to get something out of them, to gain a favor, to trick them into doing something.

But for no reason? That's a different kind of good. The kind I like. And it's rare.

"Just a minute, you guys," I told my kids as I was hoping to see him again.

Then, just as I was about to give up and leave, I saw him walking out of the restrooms. He's still beaming with confidence and wearing his shirt with pride.

"I've gotta talk to him about his shirt," I told them, as they quickly rolled their eyes with a slight head tilt and a sigh.

With that, I got into his sight line, walked up to him with my own grin, and extended a fist bump while saying, "Bro—I LOVE your shirt!"

His face lit up, he fist-bumped me back and graciously said, "Man, thanks! I live by this," while he looked down at his shirt while nodding to acknowledge it. Then, he looked back at me with a grin.

And that's the moment I met Jerrod Love. Jay Love to those who know him well.

Jay wasn't just wearing some random shirt—he was wearing his life's mantra. In the ten minutes we stood there talking, he shared just how much joy he gets from helping others in his community.

"It's the best feeling in the world," he said, with a tone that truly made his words come alive. "When you can lift someone up without expecting anything in return, it's like... it's pure, you know?"

I knew.

I asked him, "What's your favorite way to help people?"

"Awe, man, that one's easy. Money," he said, without missing a beat. "People are hurting so badly right now. I look for people in my community who are struggling, and I find ways to get them money or help them with their skills."

He had me nodding along and smiling. "How do you help them with their skills?"

Jay's eyes lit up as he explained. He recruits people into unions, organizes community classes, and connects them with his network of friends who own businesses. "I set up internships... mentoring... whatever helps them get ahead. It's all about giving them tools so they can help themselves."

Listening to him 'preach,' I knew this wasn't just a philosophy for him—it was a way of life. I could tell that Jay was the kind of person who didn't just talk about making a difference—he made it happen.

As we thanked each other for the connection and fist-bumped again, he looked me in the eyes and said, "Man, I can't tell you how much it means that you stopped to ask about my shirt. It's not often people want to talk about this stuff."

Yeah, well, not only do I want to talk about it, I want to write about it and spread Jay's message.

The best part is this: Jay didn't need validation. He didn't need a reason to be good. He just simply was. And that's what really made him stand out.

Jay made his shirt come to life that day and showed me how much of an impact one person can have by simply choosing to care. He doesn't sit around waiting for opportunities to strike—he makes them happen.

Here's the thing: we can't always see how small actions can have a ripple effect across communities, but they do. The world needs more people like Jay to just show up and start helping.

So, the next time you see a chance to "be good to people for no reason," take it, for Jay's sake. That 'chance' might be the one thing needed to change someone's day, or better yet, their life.

Because when you choose to be good for no reason, the world notices. When that happens, the bandwagon effect starts. And that's when things really start getting good.

MAKING IT MATTER

Essence of the Moment

A chance encounter with a stranger's shirt sparked a lesson in selfless kindness, showing how even the simplest acts of goodwill can ripple across lives and communities. It's not about what you expect in return—it's about the joy of lifting others up.

Timeless Truths

- ☑ **Kindness Requires No Justification:** True compassion doesn't need a reason—it thrives when given freely.
- ☑ **Be the Example You Seek:** Living out your values encourages others to mirror your actions and amplify your message.
- ☑ **Every Gesture Builds Connection:** Even the smallest acts of kindness can form meaningful bonds and strengthen communities.

Bringing It Home

1. **Recognize Opportunities for Good:** Take a moment today to notice someone who might need encouragement or a helping hand. Whether it's offering a kind word, helping someone with a task, or just giving someone your undivided attention, make a conscious choice to brighten their day.
2. **Extend Your Circle:** Over the next week, consider ways to use your resources, skills, or network to help someone else succeed. Whether it's mentoring someone, sharing a helpful connection, or providing advice, find ways to empower others.
3. **Create a Culture of Care:** In the coming month, organize or participate in a small community initiative. It could be as simple as gathering friends to donate to a cause, volunteering your time, or brainstorming ways to improve a shared space. Inspire

others to join you in creating positive change, much in the same way Jay does.

Next Level Thinking

Ask yourself:
- ▷ Am I genuinely kind without expecting something in return?
- ▷ How can I create opportunities to help others in small, impactful ways?
- ▷ Who in my life or community could use a little extra support right now?
- ▷ How can I encourage others to embrace selfless kindness?

Insight to Remember

"When you can lift someone up without expecting anything in return, it's like... it's pure, you know?"
- Jay Love

45

BEYOND THE CLOSING

All we had to do was find a place to stay for a month. We had just sold our house and were waiting to close on the next one.

Simple, right?

Not so much when the closing was halfway across the country, and you have four kids who needed to finish their semesters.

We cobbled together a plan and spent nearly three weeks sleeping on couches and floors at my in-laws' house. It was cramped—new schools, restless nights, and a tiny kitchen for our growing group—but we managed. As Christmas break approached, we packed our bags and counted down the days.

Two months prior, we'd met Sherri, our real estate agent, on a whirlwind day of house hunting. She had driven us around for twelve hours, touring neighborhoods we'd never seen, laughing at life's quirks, and swapping stories. By the end of the day, we had settled on one of the homes she showed us. Something about her felt like family from the start.

With six days until closing, Sherri and her husband did something extraordinary: they offered to let us stay with them. "We've got two extra rooms," they insisted. "Come stay and get acquainted with the area."

"Are you sure?" I asked hesitantly. "We can be a lot if you're not used to having kids around."

Not only were they sure, but they insisted. Soon, we were knocking on their door, 750 miles away from all our belongings, which were still in storage.

Sherri made every effort to make us feel at home. Over the next several days, she introduced us to her friends, guided us through local shops, and gave us a crash course in rural living.

Then came the first curveball.

Our bank postponed the closing for a month due to complications beyond our control. Christmas was three days away, and we had no access to our belongings or a clear path forward.

We were, effectively, stuck.

"Don't worry about a thing," Sherri said with a calm confidence that only comes from someone deeply rooted in faith. "We've got you covered."

And she meant it. Sherri made things happen in a hurry. She helped get our kids enrolled in the local school system, assisted with numerous challenges relating to the bank documents, and made sure Christmas still felt magical.

Morning coffee on her back porch became a ritual. As the days stretched into weeks, our bond deepened, turning what began as a business relationship into something closer to family.

Fast forward to January 20th and the second curveball.

Our bank announced they needed three additional days to close. The seller refused, saying the deal would fall through if it didn't close as scheduled. We were in a race against the clock with no backup plan.

"What can we do?" Joanna asked, her voice heavy with uncharacteristic uncertainty. "We don't have a safety net."

Moments like this test your resilience, patience, and belief in humanity.

This was a Friday afternoon. The closing was to be that next Wednesday and everything needed to be in place by Tuesday. How hard can it be?

That night, I skipped dinner and began frantically reaching out to friends who might be able to help. One by one, I struck out.

By ten o'clock, with no solution in sight, I finally joined the group gathered by the fire. Sherri had invited a few friends and neighbors over to lift our spirits, and we all had a great chat. During the conversation, one said, "I might know someone who can help."

The next morning, we found ourselves sitting in a man's office we'd never met. By "we," I'm talking about the six of us, Sherri and her husband, and Sherri's friends.

With Sherri's network working behind the scenes, he agreed to put up the funds—contingent on verifying our story by Monday morning. He agreed as long as he would be paid back, in full, within 75 days.

"What on earth is happening right now?" Joanna asks, with a mixture of excitement and bewilderment. My answer didn't help her, as I was equally dumbfounded.

Two days later, after a flurry of phone calls, emails, and prayers, we got the news: the closing would proceed as planned. Relief washed over us, and we cut through the next couple of days like they were warm butter.

But then, the third curveball.

Apparently, our journey wasn't over. Our bank needed to start a new process as it was now a refinance rather than a jumbo loan.

And with that, our three-day expectation of completing everything with the bank was nixed—meaning we were now operating under a strict 75-day deadline to repay the funds or risk forfeiting the house and our 20% down payment.

Days turned into weeks, and still, no news from the bank. "Any day now," our banker would say, his voice increasingly apologetic. By day 65, the stress was intense. Half our belongings remained unpacked, and we dared not hang pictures on the walls.

Through it all, Sherri's faith was consistent. "You'll be fine," she'd say, her optimism unwavering. "I've got a good feeling about this."

On day 68, the call finally came. "We're ready to close," our banker said. Less than a week from the deadline, papers started moving, and pens began signing. At last, it was complete, and Sherri congratulated and hugged us all.

Overall, this "moment" took us nearly five months to complete. And as I looked back, I realized how pivotal Sherri's role had been. Her grace, generosity, and steadfast belief in us turned what could have been a nightmare into a testament to the power of community and faith.

You see, God puts the right people in our lives at the right time, and Sherri was one of those people. I should mention that it was an accident I contacted her to begin with—an accident that was a result of Divine intervention. But it all happened the way it did so that she would be the one to guide us—and that's precisely why this moment stands out to me.

Sherri's actions taught me that sometimes, the most incredible gifts come from unexpected places. She showed us what it means to live with grace and to extend love without expectation. For that, she will always be part of our family's story.

So here's to all the Sherri's out there—those who go out of their way to lift others up, who believe when others doubt, and who prove that kindness, faith, and generosity can truly change lives.

MAKING IT MATTER

Essence of the Moment

Life's most transformative moments often come wrapped in unexpected challenges. The people we meet and the faith we hold onto can guide us through even the most uncertain times.

Timeless Truths

- ☑ **Grace Opens Doors:** Acts of kindness and faith can turn seemingly impossible situations into opportunities for growth and connection.
- ☑ **Community Strengthens Resilience:** The right people at the right time can provide the strength and resources we need to overcome obstacles.
- ☑ **Faith Steadies Uncertainty:** Trusting in something greater than yourself can help you face even the most unpredictable turns in life.

Bringing It Home

1. **Acknowledge Support:** Take a moment today to reflect on someone who has gone out of their way to support you during a challenging time. Send them a note of gratitude or make a quick call to express your appreciation.
2. **Extend Kindness:** Look for an opportunity to be someone's "Sherri" this week. Whether it's offering help, introducing them to a helpful contact, or simply providing encouragement, find a way to extend grace to someone in need.
3. **Strengthen Relationships:** Just as Sherri opened her home and shared her community, consider inviting someone into your life this month. Whether it's a neighbor, colleague, or new friend,

look for ways to welcome and connect with them on a deeper level.

Next Level Thinking

Ask yourself:
- How have I shown gratitude for those who have helped me through tough times?
- What opportunities do I have to extend kindness and grace to others?
- How do I respond to challenges that test my patience and resilience?
- Where can I trust more in faith rather than trying to control the outcome?

Insight to Remember

"Sherri's actions taught me that sometimes, the greatest gifts come from unexpected places. She showed us what it means to live with grace and to extend love without expectation."

46

ACCIDENTAL STORYTELLERS

What's worse than reading in front of a group of elementary students? Reading in front of eight different sets of them.

I spoke with two ladies recently, and they told me about an event that was coming up. They said they'd been asked to read to fifth-graders at a church during a Thanksgiving celebration they were having.

They were hilarious. Each of them kept talking about how the other one was going to do it because it terrified them. They were genuinely apprehensive.

"No way I'm going to stand up there and read to a bunch of kids who don't want to be there," one of them exclaimed, while the other nodded in agreement. "I'm terrified of doing this."

Amid their ongoing debate over who would ultimately "take the floor," I started my own, internally. Then, I chose the path less traveled. I opted to jump into the deep end without testing the waters.

"Can I do it? That'd be so much fun!"

You know that look people give you when they don't see what you're up to? You know, the "why would you say that?" kind? Yep, both their heads were slightly cocked, and their eyes were skeptical.

"What's the book?" I asked them as they both began to smile. "I'd love to see it to get a feel for it."

They told me, and I immediately looked it up and wondered if Madonna really wrote it. As in, THE Madonna. Yep, this book, *Mr. Peabody's Apples*, is one of at least five that she did in the early 2000's as part of her series of children's books.

Who knew? Not me, that's who.

Ten minutes later, I was grinning from ear to ear. "I could totally read that book and make it fun for fifth-graders," I said, with a great deal of unfounded confidence.

"Have you ever done something like this?" one of them asked, with genuine curiosity.

"Not yet, but I'm up for a challenge—I need something new to stress about!" I replied, with a half-cocked smile and a look of uncertainty.

When we got to the church that morning we were escorted to a little classroom that seated twelve. Our first class would be arriving in about twenty minutes, and we could just make ourselves at home.

Oh, and the two ladies were there with me, and they said they'd take over if I needed them to, but that I wasn't going to need them—under any circumstances.

That gave me a good little laugh.

For the next twenty minutes, I paced back and forth. I was apprehensive, but excited. Nervous, but okay with it.

I read through the book again and laughed at some of the names of the characters. I thought about how I might engage the class, but I really had no idea.

Then, the moment arrived. The class filled up, an introduction was given, and all eyes turned to me.

At that moment, I stopped worrying about how it would go and just leaned into the fun of it. The nervousness melted away, replaced by a sense of joy and purpose I didn't expect.

And just like that, something I didn't know I would enjoy became incredibly enjoyable. Each class of twelve became a captive audience to my random voices, pitch inflection, and ad-libbing.

I'd sometimes get so into the story that I'd lose my place in the book. And while I was searching for it, I'd make up my own storyline.

It was classic!

The kids really enjoyed it when I'd ask if anyone had the same last names of the characters as I was reading. "Tommy Tittlebottom —does anyone have the last name Tittlebottom? You look like a Tittlebottom," as I'd point to one of the kids in the class.

Each class would erupt in laughter, and then I'd move to the next character and point that one out. Then, every time that character was mentioned in the book, I'd point at that person, and everyone loved it.

When I wrapped up my eighth class, I was pleasantly surprised by a question one of the ladies with the kids asked: "Do you do this for a living?"

My answer shocked her, but only because she said it looked like I'd been doing it all my life. I had no idea I would enjoy it the way I did and, frankly, that I'd get into it.

My friend Don taught me that we don't know what we don't know. I didn't know I'd enjoy something so trivial as reading a book to fifth-graders, yet I found it exhilarating.

There was just something about the laughter, engagement, and shared joy that was unexpectedly healing—it was as if, for a few hours, all the world's worries faded, replaced by the simple joy of laughter and connection.

In other words—it reminded me how deeply human it is to share moments of levity and engagement.

Sure, anyone could have read the words on those pages— that's not what mattered. What mattered was me fully committing to the moment, to the story, and to the joy of those kids.

What this moment taught me, though, was that we don't always know what we'll like and what we won't in life. I had ideas, but I was wrong—SO wrong—about how it would go. I had to experience it firsthand.

I had to feel the feels and work through the adrenaline rush in a way I've never done. I had to stumble, fumble, and laugh at myself in ways that got my audience laughing with me. I had to help them see that reading could be fun and engaging if we let it.

I didn't know what I was doing when I started. But when I finished, I knew what I had done. I saw the importance and felt the connection in a way that no one could have warned me about.

The next time you're faced with something outside your comfort zone, say yes. You might uncover a hidden joy or talent that transforms your perspective and brings connection and happiness to others.

Isn't that the kind of story worth living—and retelling—to remind ourselves what's possible when we say yes?

MAKING IT MATTER

Essence of the Moment

Taking a chance outside your comfort zone can lead to unexpected joy, connection, and growth. Sometimes, it's the smallest "yes" that creates the biggest impact in our lives.

Timeless Truths

☑ **Embrace the Unknown:** True growth begins when we step into uncharted territory.
☑ **Laughter Connects Us:** Humor and joy have the power to dissolve barriers and create meaningful connections.
☑ **Commit Fully to the Moment:** Success often lies in being present and giving your all, even when you're unsure.

Bringing It Home

1. **Say Yes to Something Small:** Step into a situation you might usually shy away from—a meeting, a conversation, or a new activity. Embrace the challenge and observe how it feels to try something new. Maybe it'll happen today?

2. **Create Joy for Others:** Find an opportunity this week to uplift someone else with humor, storytelling, or shared experiences. Make it fun and lighthearted, and notice the connection it creates.
3. **Reflect on Past "Yes" Moments:** Spend time this month identifying moments where you said yes to something unfamiliar and reflect on the growth or joy it brought. Use this as a foundation to embrace more significant challenges in the future.

Next Level Thinking

Ask yourself:
▷ What fears or hesitations hold me back from saying yes to new opportunities?
▷ How can I turn seemingly trivial tasks into moments of joy and connection?
▷ When was the last time I felt truly present in a moment? What made it special?
▷ How might stepping outside my comfort zone impact not only me but those around me?

Insight to Remember

"The next time you're faced with something outside your comfort zone, say yes. You might uncover a hidden joy or talent that transforms your perspective and brings connection and happiness to others."

47

SPARKS THAT IGNITE

Have you ever met someone who transformed the way you work—and think—in a single afternoon?

For me, that someone was Marty Robbins, a long-haired hippie kind of fella with a contagious passion for video editing, and it all started with a simple question in the Apple store.

"Do you have anything that can help streamline things for a video editor?"

For years, I'd spent time in and out of people's homes and in studios watching tapes process and render. Transferring from one medium to the next is painful and time-consuming in ways that are just mind-numbing.

Sometimes, a single question can ignite a firestorm of responses. And that's precisely what I saw happen in real-time.

"Oh yeah—I have something you HAVE to see. Do you have a few minutes?"

It wasn't just the question... it was his excitement. He was like a kid in a candy store, and he REALLY wanted to share what he knew. Though I was short on time, I was intrigued by his demeanor, so I let Joanna know what I was going to do and excused myself.

Five minutes in: I was smiling. Ten: my wheels were turning. Fifteen: I was sold.

Not just for me but for all the folks I worked with. He showed me how to streamline projects, collaborate effortlessly, and see real-time changes.

"Joanna... you have to come meet this guy," I began, my voice excited, while popping over to get her. "You're not gonna believe what he's showing me."

Marty had his own video production business on the side and showed us what kinds of projects he was working on and how much fun he was having.

In that instant, I realized Marty wasn't just introducing me to tools—he was showing me a new way to think about creativity and problem-solving.

That night, I couldn't stop smiling. I kept thinking about my conversation with Marty and how different my life could be if I could just get past one little obstacle: not knowing how to use it all.

The next day, I contacted him and asked if we could meet to discuss potential projects and what it would take to work together. I wanted to learn quickly, and I could tell he knew what he was doing —so we made a deal.

What I didn't know was how good of a teacher he would end up being. Marty's energy was magnetic, and he taught with an infectious enthusiasm, making learning an adventure.

I didn't just want things done, I wanted to know how to do them so I could help others. What better way than to go to someone who was both an expert and an over-the-top extrovert?

Within two months, I learned the software and worked through several projects alongside him. It was the ultimate "teach a man to fish" moment for me. I quickly went from relying on others to do all the heavy lifting to laying down my own tracks and doing it the way I wanted.

Marty didn't just light a fire, he gave it the oxygen it needed to burn indefinitely. Because that's what actual teaching does—it helps someone transform an ordinary moment into a new way of thinking.

It allows them to see the world from a different perspective with new tools so they can interact differently. The physical tools (like the hardware and software) were tangible solutions I needed. But the mental tools (rethinking workflows, embracing creativity, and finding joy in efficiency) were truly what transformed the way I worked.

Marty was a Godsend. He didn't just solve our workflow frustrations, he reshaped the way we approached our projects and our timelines.

And more than that, he helped me unlock a new way of thinking—one that would ripple through every aspect of my work from that day forward.

Meeting Marty was more than an encounter—it was a reminder that teachers are all around us, ready to ignite change if we're open to it.

This moment taught us something even greater—when we find teachers who are genuinely passionate about their craft, we should embrace their energy and learn from them. Allowing them to do what they do best helps provide meaning to their lives while enhancing someone else's.

People like Marty are rare, but their impact is unforgettable. Their authenticity and passion leave a mark on everyone they meet. And if you happen to ever need someone for corporate video, look Marty up and tell him you read his story—you'll have an instant connection. You can find him at rabidrobotstudios (dot com), and he's worth connecting with.

So, here's the thing: when someone like Marty crosses your path, don't let their energy pass you by. Embrace their passion, absorb their wisdom, and let their spark ignite something extraordinary within you—just as Marty's did for me.

MAKING IT MATTER

Essence of the Moment

Transformation often begins with an unexpected encounter. Marty's passion for his craft didn't just provide tools, it reshaped how I thought, worked, and approached creativity.

Timeless Truths

- ☑ **Passion Inspires Change:** When someone brings authentic enthusiasm to their work, it can ignite transformation in others.
- ☑ **Teaching Goes Beyond Knowledge:** True teaching equips us with tools—both physical and mental—that change how we see the world.
- ☑ **Learning Opportunities Are Everywhere:** The most profound lessons often come from unexpected people and places.

Bringing It Home

1. **Look for the Spark:** Identify someone in your life who exudes passion for their craft. Spend a few minutes engaging with them today—ask questions, listen, and let their enthusiasm inspire you.
2. **Embrace a New Tool:** Commit to learning something new this week that could improve how you work or think. Whether it's a skill, a mindset, or a piece of technology, dive in with curiosity and purpose.
3. **Teach What You've Learned:** Share your knowledge or a skill you're passionate about with someone else by the end of the month. By teaching, you reinforce your understanding while inspiring others to grow.

Next Level Thinking

Ask yourself:

▷ Who in my life inspires me with their passion, and how can I learn from them?

▷ Am I open to finding lessons in unexpected places and people?

▷ What tools—physical or mental—could help me approach my work or life more creatively?

▷ How can I share my passions in ways that empower and transform others?

Insight to Remember

"Marty didn't just light a fire—he gave it the oxygen it needed to burn indefinitely. Because that's what actual teaching does—it helps someone transform an ordinary moment into a new way of thinking."

48

SAYING GOODBYE

What do you do when someone you love tells you they have less than three months to live?

I'll never forget the moment Ms. Bonnie shared the news. Heat flashed over me, my throat tightened, and I felt like I'd been sucker-punched—no way this was really happening.

"Okay," I said, with my voice trembling. "Let's look at getting a second opinion and get you set up with some alternative doctors—there's so many out there that can help."

What Bonnie couldn't see was me frantically starting to look through my notes to find her people who could help. How I began searching high and low for something—anything—that would make her life a little easier.

"I'm so tired, Shawn. I'm tired of the hatred, politics, and sickness—what has happened to our world?"

Our conversation continued, but I could tell her mind was focused on what was coming up for her and what it would mean.

The moment the doctor shared the news with her, Bonnie shifted her priorities. The moment she shared her priorities with me, my perspective changed—completely.

Through her tears, she tried to ease my mind. "Please don't worry about me," she said softly. "I'm going to be just fine."

It was hard to respond, but my silence opened her back up. "I've lived a wonderful life. I'm ready to be with Jesus, my Mama, Dad, and my grandparents."

Then, something powerful through her saddened, weakened voice hit hard: "I just want to be with my family now. To savor the time I have left, to laugh with them, and to let them know how much they mean to me."

The rest of our conversation was relatively short. Bonnie told me how proud she was that I had completed *Cherry Picking the Good* and hoped it would make a difference to others. She encouraged me to keep writing and asked me to keep sending her stories as she loved reading them in the middle of the night. Something about my stories provided her comfort when she couldn't sleep.

Shortly thereafter, our conversation ended with the familiar "Love you!"—but this time, it wasn't routine. It carried a sobering, heartfelt tone that felt like a final goodbye.

I hung up the phone but couldn't let it go. I sat there quietly and slowly absorbed the weight of everything she'd just said.

I shared the story with my family that night as I was still emotional about it. Bonnie had been like my second mom for over thirty years and someone I genuinely enjoyed sharing my life stories with.

I felt sadness for her while I was comforted by her words. And truthfully, I couldn't help feeling a tinge of envy—how many people truly get the chance to live a life so full?

Amidst the sadness and envy, another realization surfaced that brought clarity and perspective. So many people leave this world without the chance to say goodbye, unaware their time is ending.

What a rare and precious gift it is to live a life as full as hers—and to be given the time to focus on what truly matters. It doesn't ease the pain for those left behind, but it does allow for moments of connection—moments that wouldn't happen otherwise and that others will treasure.

Bonnie's presence taught me so much about kindness, compassion, and love. The kind of love she often talked about that Jesus gave: unconditional. I always admired how much she truly enjoyed her family and bragged on them as though they were running the world—because, in her eyes, they were.

Her unwavering faith and love were gifts, and I feel privileged to have witnessed them firsthand. She didn't just live a good life; she inspired others—including me—to embrace kindness and faith with open arms.

Our conversation that day was a moment in and of itself. A moment I'll treasure as it marked the end of a friendship here on earth, but it gave me a new perspective—one that allowed me to see the importance of prioritizing those we love in a whole new light.

Because, at the end of our days, those we surround ourselves with matter. Bonnie's at peace now with the rest of those she loved, and that brings me comfort.

I'm forever thankful for Ms. Bonnie's love and her lessons. She didn't just teach me the value of kindness, compassion, and family; she showed me how to live it every day. Her lessons will echo in my life and in the lives of everyone she touched.

MAKING IT MATTER

Essence of the Moment

Saying goodbye is never easy, but it offers clarity about what truly matters: love, connection, and the time we share with those we hold dear.

Timeless Truths

- ☑ **Time is a Gift:** Knowing our time is limited allows us to focus on what truly matters and make every moment count.
- ☑ **Love Leaves a Legacy:** The love we give and the relationships we nurture endure long after we're gone.
- ☑ **Faith Provides Strength:** In life's most challenging moments, faith offers comfort, clarity, and purpose.

Bringing It Home

1. **Share Your Love:** Take a moment, today, to tell someone close to you how much they mean to you. Whether through a heartfelt conversation, a note, or a small act of kindness, express your appreciation for their presence in your life.
2. **Prioritize Connection:** Set aside some time this week to be fully present with someone you love. It could be a family meal, a phone call with a distant friend, or a walk with a loved one—what matters is your undivided attention.
3. **Create a Lasting Memory:** Plan an intentional experience with those you cherish. It could be a family outing, a heartfelt letter, or even documenting shared memories through photos or a journal. Make it something they'll treasure. The sooner the better—aim for the end of the month.

Next Level Thinking

Ask yourself:

▷ How am I prioritizing the people who matter most in my life?

▷ What small actions can I take to express unconditional love today?

▷ Am I living in a way that aligns with my faith and values?

▷ What steps can I take to create meaningful connections and leave a legacy of love?

Insight to Remember

"Her unwavering faith and love were gifts, and I feel privileged to have witnessed them firsthand. She didn't just live a good life; she inspired others—including me—to embrace kindness and faith with open arms."

49

MISFIT TOYS

I t was the awards ceremony for the end of the year. Students, parents, and teachers filled the bleachers while cheering and clapping. I was right there in the mix.

I watched as all sorts of awards for grades went out, including those on honor roll for the entire year. Then, a much shorter list, but this time, just those who had straight A's.

When they ended each of those, my daughter just looked at me and smiled. I knew she had a single C, so I shrugged my shoulders, cocked my head to the side, and smiled back. I could see that she wasn't bothered IN THE LEAST.

Then, they gave subject-specific awards. I was hopeful for her. She gets pretty into each subject, and the teachers have talked about how involved she is, but nope. One by one, award by award, she sat there disappointed.

I've seen this look before. I mean, come on, I have four kids. I've seen thousands of awards go through. Sometimes they get one, sometimes they get two. Sometimes they get none.

They're not meaningless, but the truth is, they're not monumental in the scheme of things, although they definitely mean something in the moment. Especially to the kids who are receiving them. It feels good. A moment to celebrate. A smile. A picture. A pat on the back. A brief "look at my child" moment on social media. A quick mention on the phone to a grandparent or a close family friend.

I've been there. Many times.

I get it. I really do. I have a scrapbook of those kinds of "moments" from when I was a kid. It felt like they were going to matter. And, maybe they did... maybe not... it's hard to tell.

And it really is a great way to get many people involved. Truthfully, I'm not downplaying it at all, but rather, thinking of the significance, and it kinda' gets lost in the noise.

Nonetheless, she sat and watched all these awards go through and celebrated those who received them. She clapped. She cheered. She shouted their names. She was genuinely thrilled for them.

"And the 7th-grade Super Science award for Ms. So-and-So's class goes to..."

"And the 7th-grade Happy History award for Mr. Such-and-Such's class goes to..."

"And the 7th-grade Teacher's Pet for Mrs. Humpty Dumpty's class goes to..."

You know, that kind of thing. Times about fifty.

But, then, nearing the end...

My daughter's all-time favorite teacher, Mrs. Deaton, grabbed the microphone and started telling a story. About five seconds into the story, I got the chills, and my mind alerted me to the fact that this award was worth listening to.

This one sounded meaningful in a different way.

As quickly as I could, I grabbed my phone and fumbled through my password, then to the camera app, then to the video screen, and then started recording... in the hopes that my intuition was correct.

It was.

My daughter ended up receiving the "Island of Misfit Toys" award. An award created specifically to celebrate the fact that the recipient cares about others, collects people from all walks of life who are struggling or feel left out, has friends from all different friend groups, and genuinely loves people for who they are.

And there I sat with a mixed bag of emotions. Part of me was thrilled, and the other part was proud. All of me felt content.

I'm so glad someone took the time to notice that someone else takes the time to notice. You feel me?

My daughter, with all her flaws and randomness at home, does, in fact, make a whole lot of others feel really special and that they belong. My daughter knows what it's like to be hurt by friends and disappointed regularly by friends who are just horrible at her age.

And because of those things, she makes it a priority to ensure others don't get left out. That they have someone include them. That they get introduced to others. That they don't have to sit alone. That they feel welcomed at all times.

Sure, she could have received all the other awards, and I might have had a brief moment of happiness. I might have thought she was the "best" at everything for a short time... until the next time... but it didn't go like that.

Instead, she received a humanity award. An award I'll never forget, as it'll be a part of one of my all-time favorite moments. One that shined a spotlight on a young lady for shining a spotlight on others. One that highlighted who she is as a person, as a daughter, as a friend, and as a fellow human being.

So, today, I'll celebrate all those out there making the world a better place for those who struggle to be seen, included, and welcomed. We're all important and deserve to feel the kind of love this award showcased.

Congratulations, kiddo, and thanks for giving us all something to live up to.

MAKING IT MATTER

Essence of the Moment

Celebrating achievements is great, but recognizing someone for their heart and humanity is truly remarkable. The "Island of Misfit Toys" award reminded me that kindness and inclusion are the real victories in life.

Timeless Truths

☑ **Character Shines Brightest:** Skills and grades may open doors, but a compassionate heart builds bridges that last a lifetime.

☑ **Notice the Unseen:** Recognizing those who make others feel valued can be the most meaningful acknowledgment of all.

☑ **Kindness Knows No Limits:** Extending a hand to others, especially those who feel left out, creates a ripple effect of belonging and connection.

Bringing It Home

1. **Recognize Small Acts:** Start today by noticing and praising someone for a small act of kindness you see. Acknowledge it with sincerity and gratitude.
2. **Celebrate Someone's Humanity:** Take a moment this week to highlight the unique ways someone in your life makes others feel valued. Whether through a heartfelt note, a conversation, or a social media shoutout, let them know they're truly appreciated.
3. **Model Inclusion:** Make a conscious effort this month to create inclusive environments in your circles. Introduce people, invite someone new to join an activity, or simply be mindful of those who might feel left out.

Next Level Thinking

Ask yourself:
- What can I do today to make someone feel included or valued in my community?
- How can I better recognize and celebrate the unique strengths and kindness of those around me?
- What steps can I take to demonstrate inclusivity and compassion in my daily interactions?
- How can I improve the way I support and uplift others, especially those who may feel overlooked or left out?

Insight to Remember

"So, today, I'll celebrate all those out there making the world a better place for those who struggle to be seen, included, and welcomed. We're all important and deserve to feel the kind of love this award showcased."

IN A MOMENT

A lot can happen in a moment. As we've seen throughout this book, lives can be changed, lessons can be learned, friendships can be made, and hearts can be broken.

There's no shortage, really. Any moment of any given day can turn into one of your most significant—and you may not even realize it. It might be the last time you speak to someone, the song that was playing during "whatever," the month, day, and year that will forever pop up in your memories.

We don't know how it ends, but we have to show up in ways that allow us to be a part of others' stories as well. Our energy matters, our words matter, and so do our actions. Each one is a contributing factor in creating moments worth remembering.

Friends, I wrote *The Power of Moments* with the intent of sharing stories of my "moments" in a very personal way. My hope was to allow you enough insight to fully grasp each of the stories and take something from them. I wanted my "moments" to mean something at the end of the day, and for my life experiences to matter. Don't we all want that?

We all have moments that have shaped us, and we all have stories worth sharing. The trick is for you to dig deep enough and find the hidden meaning in your own. Maybe you have stories others could benefit from? I'm probably one of the people who could use them.

So the next time you're out, start creating moments that just might end up in your book. Spark conversations. Listen with intent. Be present. Teach what you've learned. Take a leap of faith. Encourage someone's effort. Celebrate someone's humanity. Be someone's mirror. Build bridges.

The way I see it is this: if we can all work together to be the good, find the good, and share the good, then the world we create becomes a much better place for everyone. All of it takes action though, and that's where you come in.

For me, writing books is just one way of connecting in a world that is anything but. To an audience that is increasingly difficult to reach on social media. With a message of hope and stories that encourage experiences and how they can change us.

My hope is that something in this book sparks something deep inside you. Where it evokes an emotion that transcends boundaries and encourages you to talk about it with others, share it online, or take some type of positive action.

Really though, thank you for taking the time to read the stories of my moments. Though they're insignificant in the scheme of things, all of them matter because they're part of a greater story —my own. You have yours and I can't wait to see and read about it with you one day.

With that, please join me in looking for and sharing *The Power of Moments* with others—in ways that only you can!

Thank you, truly,

ABOUT THE AUTHOR

Shawn Trautman has always been more interested in what drives people than in what simply moves them.

Over the last three decades, he's been the leader in more rooms than he can count—classrooms, boardrooms, locker rooms, editing rooms, control rooms, and living rooms—and across each, he's stayed grounded in the same truth: every moment tells a story, and every story holds a lesson.

Shawn's work blends clarity, movement, and purpose into tools that help people shift perspective, create impact, and move forward with intention. Whether he's teaching beginners to dance, coaching teams through transformation, or guiding leaders through critical decisions, he's always working behind the scenes to help others step into their potential—and stay there.

He's the author of *Cherry Picking the Good*, *Leadership Secrets*, *Picture Yourself Dancing*, and more than 50 full-length instruction videos focused on confidence, connection, and growth.

For Shawn, the moments we create speak louder than the goals we set. They become the stories people remember—and the legacy we leave behind.

"Moments don't just happen. We create them—by how we show up, what we say, and what we choose to see."